Electronic
Health Records

Electronic Health Records

An Audit and Internal Control Guide

Rebecca S. Busch

WILEY

John Wiley & Sons, Inc.

This book is printed on acid-free paper. ∞

Copyright © 2008 by John Wiley & Sons, Inc. All rights reserved.
Published by John Wiley & Sons, Inc., Hoboken, New Jersey.
Published simultaneously in Canada.

For general information on our other products and services, or technical support, please contact our
Customer Care Department within the United States at 800-762-2974, outside the United States at
317-572-3993 or fax 317-572-4002.

Wiley also publishes its books in a variety of electronic formats. Some content that appears in print may
not be available in electronic books.

For more information about Wiley products, visit our Web site at http://www.wiley.com.

Library of Congress Cataloging-in-Publication Data:

Busch, Rebecca S.
  Electronic health records : an audit and internal control guide / Rebecca S. Busch.
    p. cm.
  Includes index.
  ISBN 978-0-470-25820-0 (cloth : alk. paper)
    1. Medical records—Data processing. 2. Medical audit. 3. Electronic records—Access
control. I. Title.
    [DNLM: 1. Forms and Records Control—methods. 2. Medical Records Systems,
Computerized—organization & administration. 3. Access to Information. 4. Management
Audit. 5. Medical Audit. W 80 B977e 2008]
  R864.B87 2008
  651.5'04261—dc22
                                                                        2008017689

Printed in the United States of America
10 9 8 7 6 5 4 3 2 1

To Samantha, Andy, and Albert, my daily source of inspiration

Contents

Preface

The reasonable man adapts himself to the world; the unreasonable man persists in trying to adapt the world to himself. Therefore, all progress depends on the unreasonable man.

—GEORGE BERNARD SHAW (1856–1950), IRISH WRITER

I have so many reasons for writing this book. First, it served as a personal exercise to organize my thoughts on the subject. Second, I wanted to explore what is needed to achieve a paperless healthcare environment. What changes will need to occur to achieve interoperability among all the market players? What does this all really mean, and how do we in the healthcare industry continue to work within the various market initiatives during our day-to-day jobs? Clearly, a key component to all of this is *change*. That is the theme throughout this book.

What types of changes are occurring and being introduced by various market players? *How* will the parties achieve such change and manage the existing environment while in transition? *Where* will these changes take place in our current healthcare system? *Who* will be affected by all these changes? *When* will these changes take place? Ultimately, *why* are these changes taking place? *Why* is key, because we cannot improve without change. We cannot move forward without change. At times, the suggested changes and requirements will appear to be unreasonable as we try to adapt the world toward a new direction. At first glance, the initiatives that generate progress will no doubt appear to be unreasonable.

In preparing this book, I selected several areas to cover. The first is a general review of the electronic and digital healthcare world. Next is a review of various market initiatives that are setting the stage for change. To initiate change, organizations, such as the Agency on Healthcare Research and Quality, develop infrastructures to gather intelligence for best-practice models from available clinical information. E-health provides hope to these organizations and others that require efficient access to this information to optimize their efforts.

In the electronic world, activity happens fast—either efficiently and effectively fast or disastrously and deadly fast. I selected to focus on the Department of Defense Records Management System because its standards provide a great foundation for the functional aspects of records management software. I have included analysis of the involvement of several other organizations because they help provide insight into market changes and directions. The omission of any group, organization, or initiative is by no means a statement of the lack of value or importance.

As I progressed in organizing my thoughts, it was helpful to understand how people were using health information, especially nontraditional users of health information. This includes both legitimate and illicit market players. When one thinks about health information, the first player that comes to mind is usually the patient. However, health information has many users.

My research also included several market conflicts. One of particular interest is the concept of *case management*. I truly believe that the market has many counterproductive, conflicting monetary incentives. They are the cause behind many lobbyist efforts and resistance to change. At times, as healthcare professionals we provide healthcare advice to our patients; however, is it ever financially driven? The same is the case when a payer executes the process of precertification and denies a requested coverage based on "lack of medical necessity" with a follow-up disclaimer, "This does not mean that we are saying that your provider is providing unwarranted care." Other than leaving the consumer obviously confused and conflicted, the plausible question is, What is the incentive behind the denial of this care? As a result, one has to question the real incentive behind the directives and plans for patient care. Are directives for care driven financially or clinically? Are plans for care data driven by accepted standards?

I firmly believe that the unpleasant task of discussing how money impacts healthcare delivery is often masked. An unveiling will require fundamental changes in attitude and the recognition of financial versus clinical case management. These two disciplines are discussed in theory and application. How a payer approaches the clinical and financial case management of a patient will vary from how a provider will approach these two disciplines. In fact, the entire healthcare continuum (HCC) responds to these issues differently.

In a previous publication, *Healthcare Fraud Audit and Detection Guidebook*, I introduced the market players of the HCC. In this publication, I subdivide this HCC concept into three layers. As presented in *Healthcare Fraud Audit and Detection Guidebook,* the primary HCC of users includes the patient, the provider, the third-party payer, the plan sponsor, and all the support vendors. The introduction of the secondary HCC of users includes activities outside of direct and indirect patient case activity such as research, monitoring, and respective public and private agency work. The third continuum, referred to as the *information continuum*, is the link to e-health. This continuum highlights the functional drivers behind achieving an interoperable environment. These healthcare continuums are covered in more detail in Chapter 1. Understanding this subdivision of the HCC is important in appreciating the complexity in developing a truly interoperable environment.

I hope that you will find that the selection of topics in this book spawns new ideas on how to approach issues in e-health. In addition, I hope to provide a constructive guideline in developing the most appropriate approach to auditing e-health infrastructures and ongoing initiatives. Thank you and enjoy!

About the Author

Rebecca Busch, RN, MBA, CCM, CHS-III, CFE, FHFMA is the president and CEO of Medical Business Associates located in Westmont, Illinois, and at www.mbanews.com. MBA Inc. has a unique core competency in conducting technology-and process-enabled audits of healthcare claims and processing. Ms. Busch has over 100 publications and presentations, along with 20-plus years of progressive achievement in the healthcare management industry. She developed proprietary data analysis tools and currently has a patent pending on a data anomaly profiler and a second patent pending on a case management system for a personal health record (PHR) management system. She is a registered nurse and an MBA as well as a certified fraud examiner (CFE), healthcare fellow in financial management (FHFMA), and has a Master's Certificate in Case Management (CCM).

In 1991, Ms. Busch founded Medical Business Associates with the vision of delivering a multidisciplinary approach to conducting comprehensive audits for employers, providers, and insurance companies. Her proprietary methodology employs statistical analysis of claims and procedural data specifically targeted to identify the most probable areas of operational breakdowns, exposure to fraud, financial errors, and cost savings. Ms. Busch's ability to quickly identify anomalies from vast amounts of data has distinguished her and Medical Business Associates as an invaluable source enabling dramatic cost savings for clients. In addition, Ms. Busch testifies as an expert in the area of healthcare reimbursement, internal controls, life care expense analysis, patient care documentation, and respective damages. She has authored *Healthcare Fraud: Audit and Detection*

Guide (2007) and *Electronic Health Records: An Internal Audit Guide* (2008), both published by John Wiley & Sons, Inc. In addition, Ms. Busch has written a how-to guide, that will teach American families how to prevent medical errors and detect fraud in reviewing their own families' medical records through MBA's electronic personal health record, PortFolia^sm. Selected case study contributions include: "I Do" (case study on identity theft) in *Case Studies in Computer Fraud* (2008) and "Bodies for Rent" in *Fraud Casebook: Lessons from the Bad Side of Business* (2007), both edited by Joseph T. Wells and published by John Wiley & Sons, Inc. Ms. Busch is a faculty member of the Association of Certified Fraud Examiners and makes frequent public speaker appearances.

Ms. Busch has had several professional appointments:

- Expert panel member, phase 1, Department of Health and Human Services, Office of the National Coordinator of Health Information Technology for the Foundation of Research and Education of the American Health Information Management Association, of a project to explore the use of health information technology to enhance and expand healthcare antifraud activities, 2005
- Expert panel member, phase 2, of the same project to develop model antifraud requirements for electronic health records, 2006–2007
- National Insurance Crime Bureau, committee member for public awareness, subject matter expert on developing fraud awareness in the community, 2006–2008
- Testimony before the American Health Information Community regarding health information technology criteria to enhance prevention and detection of waste, fraud, and abuse, 2007
- Member of the expert panel for 2008 Health Information Exchange Practice Council, e-HIM Work Group for Medical Identity Theft
- Development of practice guidelines, American Health Information Management Association, 2008

Acknowledgments

I need to begin with a special thank-you to my editor, Timothy Burgard, for patiently listening to concepts of this book and my previous book, *Healthcare Fraud Audit and Detection Guidebook*. In addition, another special thank-you goes to Graham McNally, for many long hours reviewing chapters. I would like to also acknowledge reviews from Joe Saltiel, Scott Dolan, Jean-Francois Legault, and James Foley, for sneaking in chapters and listening patiently to concepts in between the Bears and Cubs games, and thanks to Lesley Melin for facilitating distribution and collection of e-health surveys from consumers.

I have several professional peers who have had an impact on my learning and growing insight: thanks to Reed D. Gelzer, MD, MPH, CHCC, for ongoing academic banter on all subjects related to e-health and healthcare waste, fraud, and abuse; Marie Stanley, a very longtime provider audit mentor; Craig Greene, a very longtime *forensic audit* mentor; and Jerry Roush, a longtime internal audit mentor. I am also grateful for the opportunities of professional participation within the Association of Certified Fraud Examiners and the International Institute of Internal Auditors, which opened doors and provided a foundation of skills to tackle this and other topics.

I need to include several long-term and current employees, including but not limited to Mary Glynn, Donna Graham, and Janet McManus, who patiently followed the train ride with absolute confidence, although not always knowing the direction. They modeled the acceptance of change and perseverance with a great work ethic and roll-them-sleeves-up and let's-get-our-hands-dirty attitude.

During the past two years, I had the opportunity to work on several committees initiated by the Department of Heath & Human Services—Healthcare/Health IT. The discussion among these two panels of experts was insightful and very rewarding.

Since 1991, when I founded MBA Inc., our audit work throughout the healthcare continuum has provided ongoing insight into the need for change. I would like to thank our clients, who trusted our efforts and were indeed open to change, the theme driving the work of this book. A thank-you also goes out to Patricia Farrer, whose need to manage the complex healthcare system inspired the development of a healthcare portfolio that has developed into MBA's e-PHR offering, PortFolia^{sm}, to empower herself and other patients to self-advocate. Finally, I need to thank my children, family, and friends for their continued support of my non–beach novel writings!

Here is a special song for all of you involved in persevering in interoperable e-health. This was written by a friend who chooses to remain anonymous!

The Compliance Blues

(Sung to a bluesy riff, like George Thorogood's "Bad to the Bone")

You see this frown on my face and I am dragging my feet;

I just came from another client meet and greet . . .

They just bought themselves one of them ole . . . *Eee Em Arrs*;

Now can you please direct me to the nearest bar.

I got the compliance blues, from head to my shoes,

Oh Lord, please spare me from paying more dues.

I'm getting so tired of telling all these fools

That just because it's on a computer it cannot break all the rules.

Last week I met a doctor, told me what a great system he got;

If the payer don't like the record he just changes it like a shot.

He deletes the nurses' notes when they make him look bad;

He's just so damned happy to be part of this EMR fad.

I got the compliance blues, from head to my shoes,

Oh Lord, please spare me from paying more dues.

I'm getting so tired of telling all these fools

That just because it's on a computer it cannot break all the rules.

The administrator loves it, it is so eeeficient and fast;

The MA's see the all patients and the docs don't even walk past.

The EMR signs all the notes by the doc;

Everyone gets paid great, the notes are solid as rock.

I got the compliance blues, from head to my shoes,

Oh Lord, please spare me from paying more dues.

I'm getting so tired of telling all these fools

That just because it's on a computer it cannot break all the rules.

I saw a dictation system just the other day,

That makes reviewing records easy, to get them out of the way.

You don't even have to read them, it wraps them up in a ball,

And you just hit a button and you've signed them all.

I got the compliance blues, from head to my shoes,

Oh Lord, please spare me from paying more dues.

I'm getting so tired of telling all these fools

That just because it's on a computer it cannot break all the rules.

I think I am going to quit this auditing game;

I am tired of ending each day drunk and ashamed.

What keeps me going to the next place I'll arrive

Is if I make one record worth trusting it may keep someone alive.

I got the compliance blues, from head to my shoes,

Oh Lord, please spare me from paying more dues.

I'm getting so tired of telling all these fools

That just because it's on a computer it cannot break all the rules.

Introduction

We will make wider use of electronic records and other health information technology to help control costs and reduce dangerous medical errors.

—President George W. Bush, January 31, 2006

Euoiweuowueoupouv opuweoiurou iiHOJUPiOIUOWUoijeojiojeo-jaeijoija mvoiueomviueowirtvaoiwetovwietbonuaweiotuioeuioeunjovu weorvweoimroewiubn eoiurnoiewunroewiunvowei. V oaiweuoiueb ounouwouowueoau pouaeiopou u u89wuwe oiaweaoi 93w9u o u 308un398 oiajpoweu 9. pw0985v938nv 98nvp032uvjwnvp93r4p93 uoivrewjkfreav/v.v. !# aoweoiuaoiuoi opiuoieowja j ;jewoaj;oijeoiajewfoij oieu98v0943rvm09m ivqp93wrv903rv09w3;ou3wp9ivl.v9i0/V9I9?VIWEOIU OO V OIAUER PWUVM03QU9ROVUOWUV MNVBMJI;oipiew9iv v9uop9uweov.. v[9iwaeo9uv oi h v;ouiaewoiutuivu 1240/982398 v9aqwp90ourm9 uv r3our3wv c cvwoumuv3 u43v,nr3wv 9u nur4w o,uiwvr9pm9wbt4.

If you can discern *who, what, when, where, why*, and *how* from the above paragraph, then set this book aside. You will not need it. Walk confidently into your next healthcare audit, because you have passed your first audit test in the e-health world by believing that all available and appropriate information is quickly at hand. This is the wrong assumption to make! If you cannot make sense of the first paragraph, then continue reading.

If you have never had the experience of auditing or attempting to use an electronic record output like the first paragraph, then you have not experienced the front line as an e-health post-care user of information.

The output shown in the first paragraph is from a hospital's electronic record system. The program that the hospital purchased did not come with a function that allowed an electronic file transfer of a record to another electronic medium. In other words, the first paragraph is what it looked like when the user tried to save the electronic record to a DVD. As a result, the user had to print the record to paper. The program did not make this function easy at all. To print this same electronic record into paper form required three hours of labor at a computer to call up each section of a five-day hospital stay. The software developers who developed the program purchased by the hospital evidently did not take into consideration that copies of medical records need to be forwarded in electronic or hardcopy form. As a result, when the medical records department responded to a request for a copy of records, it became a very labor-intensive task.

Electronic Health Records: An Audit and Internal Control Guide reviews today's complex and fragmented healthcare e-information marketplace. This guidebook introduces various audit and internal control principles that can be applied and modified as the market moves into a true interoperable functional state. The term *interoperable* in the context of healthcare records describes electronic healthcare record systems that communicate and work together. Hospital providers currently may have one type of system for maintaining a patient's records, patients may have another electronic system, insurance companies may use a third type of system, and so forth. These systems are *not* interoperable; they do not communicate or work with each other.

This book looks at several different aspects of the e-health world. One aspect explores how the healthcare system is broken up into at least three areas: functional communications, clinical accountability, and financial accountability. Another aspect explores how the healthcare system uses electronic systems only part of the time; these electronic systems in turn are fragmented, poorly integrated, and convoluted at the functional, clinical, and financial level. A third aspect explores how the market is aggressively moving these same broken and convoluted systems into an interoperable e-health world without addressing clinical and financial accountability in the delivery of healthcare services.

Computer vendors currently sell electronic healthcare systems that focus a great deal on functional aspects of medical care, such as documenting patients' vitals signs while they are at the hospital and inserting pictures of the x-rays directly into the electronic patient record. These electronic systems, however, fall short on post-care delivery operational functions, such as the ability to print final records and retrieve billing information for episodes of care once an account is closed. This year, for example, I audited a medical practice that had purchased a well-established electronic system that did not allow users to easily retrieve closed claims activities. Amazingly, the system automatically purged closed accounts. How can anyone provide retrospective audits and monitor for both clinical and financial outcomes without this basic function? Certain aspects of data access within our broken clinical and financial systems will remain the same unless we change issues fundamental to the delivery and financing of healthcare.

This book serves as a guide to gather data intelligence from within the current operating system's framework. Valuable interim data can be obtained from this framework that will help us better understand healthcare costs and minimize the risk of medical errors. Setting up appropriate internal controls will help achieve some level of valuable output regardless of infrastructure. The ability to gather data intelligence depends on an understanding of the mechanics of a particular system and then the methodology developed to abstract such information. Finally, it is important to recognize what needs to be changed, upgraded, or removed to empower future e-health environments to maximize intelligence.

Healthcare delivery systems are costly for government plan sponsors, public and private employers, individual patients, providers of care, vendors that support the healthcare market, and third-party payers of care. This book includes a working interactive health information record management system application for individual patients. The tool originated out of Medical Business Associates, Inc.'s advocacy activity on behalf of patients. Such activities include selecting healthcare services, managing clinical and financial information, and, ultimately, being a self-advocate in preventing or mitigating financial and clinical errors, or even outright fraud.

The book also provides information on key market activities within the Department of Health and Human Services. This agency has been developing criteria for e-health and individual health records. Based on the mission statement set forth by President Bush in 2006, significant market initiatives have already taken place and will continue. The pilot for Medicare beneficiaries was initiated in 2007. Medicaid has initiated additional activities with respect to cost control activities. Both public programs have initiated activities specifically to address waste, fraud, and abuse in the e-health environment. The public programs traditionally set the benchmark for the private market.

The use of personal health records for employees is also a timely topic and an ongoing issue from an operational perspective. Personal healthcare record management systems—whether for group health coverage, workers' compensation cases, Medicare beneficiaries, or Medicaid recipients—will evolve as a control point for the efficacy of healthcare-related clinical and financial activities. The focus and discussions in this book are on the content infrastructure of electronic health records and on how the government's criteria and other emerging professional market standards impact the private and public marketplaces.

Using This Book

This book begins with an overview of the market. What exactly is e-health? How do tools such as the Internet, intranets, or digital versus electronic information come into play? How is health information, regardless of form, even generated? Who are its authors, keepers, and users? The primary focus in Chapter 1 is on the content and the impact that this content has on the marketplace.

Chapter 2 begins with an overview of public and private uses of health information. It then discusses several key market movements on standards, including those by various organizations that have unique perspectives on and make important contributions to e-health initiatives. For example, the Agency for Healthcare Research and Quality (AHRQ) is a not-for-profit professional organization whose initiatives include data-driven outcome research information for clinical decision making. AHRQ efforts are impacted by the optimal generation of e-healthcare data. Another organization, Health Level Seven, Inc. (better known as HL7), is an internationally based, not-for-profit organization that strives, through collaboration, to create standards for the exchange and integration of electronic health information. HL7 has been progressive in developing various market standards to achieve effectiveness and efficiency of healthcare delivery information systems. Another set of market standards is the Department of Defense Directive 5015.2 (the DOD Records Management Program).

Chapter 2 next reviews initiatives created by the Association of Records Managers and Administrators (ARMA). ARMA's efforts focus on how information management, whether in electronic or paper format, is a key to doing business. Chapter 2 ends with a discussion of the e-health standards being introduced by the Certification Commission for Healthcare Information Technology (CCHIT).

Chapter 3 reviews a market conflict that Medical Business Associates, Inc. has identified in the course of auditing providers, payers, employers, and vendors within the healthcare market. That conflict has to do with the concept of case management of an individual's health. A professional organization known as the Case Management Society of America (CMSA) defines *case management* as "a collaborative process of assessment, planning, facilitation and advocacy for options and services to meet an individual's health needs through communication and available resources to promote quality cost-effective outcomes." The market problem concerns how each healthcare market player applies its own definition of case management.

The collaborative process involving clinical and financial issues is integrated, but not always separated as financial versus clinical issues, nor does it always work effectively. Take a simple example: a patient is offered a treatment plan that includes only what is covered by the insurance company rather than the latest type of treatment for his or her disease. Chapter 3 separates these two types of behaviors. The clinical case management plan should include the most appropriate treatment plan. The financial case management plan should identify what the patient will pay for and what is covered by the patient's insurance policy. It should also include the patient's financing options if he or she chooses not to go with the policy provisions. The point in suggesting that the market separate the two disciplines is to provide the patient the opportunity to make an informed decision. I see the lack of separation as a market conflict. As the market progresses into a truly interoperable electronic world, expect the financial and clinical sides of the business to collide and lingering conflicts to come into full view.

Chapter 4 introduces the concept of data in and of itself and the dynamics of the elements and a methodology to sort and identify information. Chapter 5 leads into a detailed discussion on algorithms— the types of formulas utilized to drive the data elements. Chapter 6 initiates the concept of data-driven health decisions and responds to the question of how intelligence is derived and/or attempted electronic infrastructures in the e-health world. How can we maximize the usefulness of information with e-health technology? Chapter 7 follows with the development of analytic tools and audit checklists to ensure appropriate internal controls. Chapter 8 reviews what the market is currently offering and provides a comparison on how the vendors are contributing to the direction of e-health developments and market conflicts. Chapter 9 provides a more patient-focused perspective on the personal health record. Finally, the book ends with a discussion on the substance behind electronic health records and personal health records, followed by a discussion on listening to our customers—the ultimate key to success!

This book's focus—what to look for in an e-health system with respect to content and e-health's impact on both direct and indirect patient care and direct and indirect operational support functions—makes it different from guidebooks that walk you through the security and technical infrastructures. This book addresses the question, How do you audit for content, infrastructure, and process of a health information system? It then details audit tools and future considerations for continued internal controls.

CHAPTER 1

Market Background

Change is the law of life. And those who look only to the past or present are certain to miss the future.

—JOHN F. KENNEDY (1917–1963),
THIRTY-FIFTH PRESIDENT OF THE UNITED STATES

E-HEALTH

What is *e-health?* Is it merely a fashionable buzzword from the 1990s? Is it a new way for marketing professionals to distinguish their healthcare offerings, or just a way for them to repackage their old offerings? E- (electronic-) health is all about technology. *E-information* is today's revolutionary market tool across all industry sectors. The term *tools* is used in the context of electronic processing of a particular operation. It is the technology of communicating, processing, and deriving information in electronic form. E-information will continue to impact the healthcare industry. Although the market players (patients, providers, payers, plan sponsors, and other third-party service providers) within the *healthcare continuum* (HCC) remain intact, how each functions within the continuum along with their diagnostic tools and treatment protocols continues to change.

What has changed? What is new? E-health initiatives essentially implement new, evolving forms of electronic communication and processing tools in our current healthcare system. As e-health initiatives continue to emerge, we may learn better ways to redefine the roles of our market players. In fact, we should expect some traditional roles and processes to continue to change in scope as technology modernizes the healthcare industry.

Evidenced-based medicine is being presented as an e-health opportunity. Evidenced-based medicine can be defined as

> The conscientious, explicit and judicious use of current best evidence in making decisions about the care of individual patients. The practice of evidence-based medicine requires the integration of individual clinical expertise with the best available external clinical evidence from systematic research and our patient's unique values and circumstances.[1]

The key e-health initiative would be the assimilation of *external* clinical evidence. Most providers are creating internal electronic systems to be more efficient within their organizations. Providing structure to health clinical outcomes from external sources would impact how we make decisions in healthcare. The audit concerns would revolve around ensuring the security and integrity of the external information being integrated with internal evidence. This opportunity should be developed within a contemporaneous internal audit control environment.

We often hear the term *efficiency* directly correlated to e-health. If someone needs to obtain a prior medical record of a patient in a traditional paper record system, it requires physically going into a file room. If someone needs to study how a patient or a series of patients responded to a treatment plan, she must engage in a set of manual processes to achieve a certain level of intelligence from the information. In other words, because a paper system is manually driven, it requires more labor hours to arrive at a particular outcome.

E-health initiatives provide the opportunity to reduce the labor associated with the retrieval of healthcare information. Similarly, electronic tools that sift through large amounts of data at a speed and consistency unmatched by any human provide the opportunity to reduce the labor associated with the processing and reading of each paper page of information.

But is there any guarantee that e-health initiatives will make all aspects of healthcare processes more efficient? In a recent audit of an e-health system, the task of organizing a patient's health information and determining what, where, when, why, and how a patient was treated clinically and financially was found to be more time consuming than that same task in a traditional paper system.

The number of e-health tools that simply do not have a clear *e-audit trail* within their systems is alarming. If a bank implemented similar types of e-financial tools, then someone could walk into its vault at any time without any tracking of his activities. The audit of a 500-bed hospital in which the new state-of-the-art e-health system had the ability to track additions and deletions of a medical record showed that the system design did not include a control to prevent a user from deleting or adding an entire medical record episode. Another 250-bed hospital purchased a system that in essence merely tracks the activity of the last user. For example, someone could enter a medical record and record a narrative. Another user could walk in behind her and rewrite her narrative, and the system would keep track of only the last entry and have no record of the original entry. On the financial side, there are systems in which the billing side will purge account activity once the account is closed. If that provider was subjected to any audits, it would have no ability to follow the money. Imagine being presented with an audit from Medicare or Medicaid that wanted last year's accounts in which claims were submitted. In your response, you would have to clarify that the system you purchased automatically purges all accounts and you can no longer retrieve the information. Having a system that leaves your organization noncompliant with the ability to audit your claims is a significant high-risk situation to be in.

E-health is about digital healthcare data in electronic form that designated market players generate, transfer, and utilize. The technology behind e-health consists of digital tools, electronic tools, and network exchanges conceived and built to facilitate the transfer of such data. One of the foremost ongoing concerns about e-health lies in the management of its technological growth. How, for example, will we manage data when the materials and equipment (hard drive storage technology) used to create that storage become obsolete? Another significant concern regarding e-health involves the effect that varying rates of technology adoption among the market players will have on the healthcare system. The concept of interoperability thus refers not only to market acceptance of electronic media utilization but also to an environment in which the market standard drives consistent use of current technological capabilities.

From an audit perspective, the critical question concerning e-health focuses on its impact on *market roles and processes*. We will examine this impact in closer detail.

How Is Electronic Information Created?

The following is a very brief overview of the history, terminology, and acceleration of developing technologies.[2] The evolution of technology provides the foundation for the auditors' information diagram in Exhibit 1.1. The latter half of the twentieth century has seen an explosion in new technology. While they may have started as government experiments or research projects, the results of the development projects have become a part of our everyday lives. Everything from television to computers to cell phones is a result of this technological revolution. We live in a digital age, and it is defined by technology and innovation. The tools used today to execute various functions within the healthcare domain are a result of this digital age. They can be classified into the following categories: electronics, computers, networks, software, and storage.

The digital age really began with the development of the transistor in 1947 by Bell Laboratories. Transistors are semiconductor devices that can manipulate electronic signals. They are the basis of all digital circuits, including microchips, which use millions of microscopic transistors to power everything from calculators to cell phones. Transistors are the building blocks of all electronics, including computers.

The transistor made building electronics faster and cheaper, and allowed manufacturers to build smaller and smaller devices. Electronics that were once the size of a room are now able to fit in the palm of our hand. The advances over the years have influenced the tools used in healthcare and have increased the accuracy and quality of healthcare. From digital thermometers to MRI machines, all aspects of healthcare are affected by the growth of electronic tools.

In speaking of electronics, one cannot ignore the most significant electronic tool: the computer. While computers predated the development of the transistor and modern electronics, those early vacuum-tubed giants were really used only in government and corporate research. With advances in digital circuits, computers became cheaper, faster, and more available than ever before.

This in turn spurred the growth of new ways to use computers as software and programming languages were created and implemented. For example, the introduction of FORTRAN (short for the *IBM Mathematical FORmula TRANslating System*) in 1957 enabled a computer to perform a repetitive task from a single set of instructions by using loops.[3] Developed in the early 1950s by the Stanford Research Institute, with funding from Bank of America, ERMA (Electronic Recording Machine Accounting) explored the automation of check handling and posting. When it went into production in 1959, Bank of America had a reliable solution to automate checking accounts. To get there, it had to overcome a number of hurdles, one of which was finding a solution to automate inputting of check information. This led to the creation of *magnetic ink character recognition*. Now checks could be preprinted with magnetic-ink font characters that could be read automatically or by humans. These are still visible at the bottom of the checks we use today. In 1960, COBOL was introduced for business use; LISP, for writing artificial intelligence languages; and Quicksort, for increasing the speed of data sorting. A few years later, the introduction of the American Standard Code for Information Interchange (ASCII) enabled machines from different manufacturers to exchange data.

Computers also had to be able to store the information they processed. In the beginning, this was done with punch cards. Advances in data storage technology grew as the need for more storage was created by the advances in computing. The more power the digital circuits or microchips had, the more processing they could do, which led to more information being processed and the need for larger storage capacity. In the 1950s, IBM introduced disk storage technology to the world when it launched the IBM 305 RAMAC, which could store 4.4 MB on 50 24-inch platters back in 1956. We have come a long way since the IBM 305 RAMAC, as *storage area networks* (networks of shared storage devices) can store terabytes of information. We carry around flash drives that hold over 4 GB and are smaller than a pack of gum.

Storage is a vital component of an auditor's checklist for any e-health system, and the ability to ensure the confidentiality, integrity, and availability of the information stored is vital.

The final piece of the puzzle was *networking*, or the ability to have computers communicate with one another. This really began in 1960, when AT&T designed the data-phone, a commercial modem that converted digital computer information into analog signals. The data-phone set the stage for a series of advancements in data transmission over the next decade. ARPANET was born in 1969, from the Defense Advanced Research Project Agency of the U.S. Department of Defense. Its goal was to enable communication between research laboratories, universities, and the military.

ARPANET was in fact the predecessor to the Internet, but it did not gain the public's attention until the early 1990s. In 1975, Telnet became the first publicly available commercial network service. Established in 1980, USENET is one of the oldest communication systems still in use today. At its inception, USENET allowed users to post and reply to public messages more than a decade before the World Wide Web by relying on the UUCP protocol to copy messages from one server to another. In 1983, the military portion of ARPANET was broken off as a separate network, MILNET. Before the break off, ARPANET was comprised of 113 nodes; today it is estimated that more than 1 billion people use the Internet. ARPANET became what we now know as the *Internet*.

The Internet is now a worldwide publicly accessible series of interconnected computer networks that exchange data using the Internet Protocol suite. The Internet Protocol suite (sometimes referred to as *TCP/IP*, based on its two most important protocols—Transmission Control Protocol and Internet Protocol) is a set of communication protocols that allow for standardized communication between hosts connected to the Internet or other private networks. The Internet serves to transport a variety of information using services like the World Wide Web and electronic mail.

The *World Wide Web*, created by Tim Berners-Lee, is comprised of a series of interlinked documents accessible via the Internet. The Hypertext Transfer Protocol (HTTP), a member of the Internet Protocol suite, allows for the transfer of information on the Web. The commercialization of the Web in the mid-1990s sparked online commerce as it allowed companies to create a presence online. Today, the Web has become a ubiquitous technology along with electronic mail.

Electronic mail, often abbreviated as *e-mail*, is a method of exchanging messages over a communication network such as the Internet. Having its roots in a variety of protocols, it allows users to compose, send, and receive messages.

Although adoption of new technology depends on the successful integration of a variety of components, it is clear that components do not evolve at the same rate. What does this mean to the healthcare industry?

Exhibit 1.1 demonstrates the categories that should be identified in the scope of auditing an information infrastructure.

From an information perspective, the auditors' assessment should include questions that help identify the current electronic infrastructure of electronic information communications. For example, a checklist of questions might include:

❏ Identify the current electronic infrastructure of information communications.
❏ Identify what computer tools are being used to communicate information.
❏ Identify what components are currently being used.
❏ Identify the process flow of the network.

EXHIBIT 1.1   INFORMATION CONTINUUM (IC)

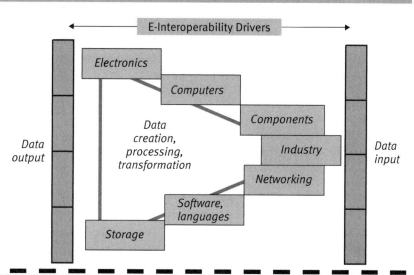

Source: MBA Inc. (www.mbanews.com; copyright 2007).

❑   What software and languages are we currently using to communicate information?

❑   What types of storage devices do we use?

For each item in the checklist, auditors should understand *why* the designated tool is used, *where* the tool is maintained, *how* the tool is implemented, and *whether* the tool uses the most appropriate framework and structure, to determine whether the information extrapolated from an e-audit will meet the standards of sufficiency and relevancy.

INFORMATION TECHNOLOGY CONSIDERATIONS

Auditing the systems and processes of an organization that utilizes information technology requires a general understanding of its technological components. In addition to a *subject matter expert*, a successful audit team will need to adopt someone who has an appropriate understanding of technological components such as operating systems, hardware, software, change or version control activities, and security devices.

An operating system is the software that allows the computer to run and process information on behalf of its user. Examples include Windows, Unix, Linux, and the Mac OS. An operating system therefore enables users to run various applications, such as an electronic healthcare record to manage information about a patient's care. Within the scope of any audit, it is important to recognize which operating system an organization uses. Your audit at minimum should include compliance with maintenance and software update requirements to help ensure the integrity of the infrastructure.

Four types of hardware exist: mainframes, servers, minicomputers, and personal computers. The *mainframe*, the original computer, is powerful and tends to connect to numerous terminals and peripheral devices. *Servers* provide infrastructure connecting the mainframe to other computer systems. These types of electronic system arrangements often include both hardware and software applications. In other words, any electronic system within any organization will include the use of hardware and software. Servers tend to serve a smaller network of users. *Minicomputers* (bigger than desktops and smaller than mainframes) are a setup of workstations that can run on a desktop and sometimes serve as a central computer for smaller organizations. *Personal computers* and *laptops* either function and stand alone or are configured for access to a defined network. Due to advances in technology, desktop personal computers can now outperform mainframe infrastructures.

Many different types of software and applications exist, and a working knowledge of the software used by the organization being audited is necessary. When looking at a personal healthcare record, consider the dynamics of merging different sources of information. *It is the process of identifying each source document and the type of software and application that is housing the information. This will be important in testing the ability for the information to be integrated.* The audit may find that some systems are not compatible with others.

Adequate controls of information technology, security measures including virus protection and firewalls, audit trails, quality assurance, and provisions for emergency changes, sourcing, and general tracking of all end-user activities will be discussed in more detail in a later chapter.

E-health initiatives accumulate databases comprised of sensitive information. These databases can be *flat* or *relational*. Flat databases incorporate all information elements into one source, whereas relational databases link a series of databases containing different information elements. How databases use and store information deserves significant attention due to privacy concerns.

Other information technology developments that require attention include e-commerce, electronic funds transfer (EFT), and enterprise resource planning (ERP). E-commerce involves conducting commercial activities over the Internet. EFT is the way electronic payments are made in e-commerce. E-commerce has become prevalent in many industries. The airline industry, for instance, is quickly developing into a virtual-world activity since the need for in-person transactions is almost obsolete. As various components of healthcare move in this direction, specific concerns will follow with respect to the extent that patient needs can and should be addressed in a virtual world.

Enterprise resource planning software is the heart of what is happening in e-health. ERP is the art of taking the entire information infrastructure from each department and their respective functions and integrating them into one system. Exhibit 1.2 illustrates the data map for one hospital. Each component electronically is operating independently from all others. Thus the task of integration requires careful planning; otherwise,

EXHIBIT 1.2

SAMPLE SEGMENTED DATA MAP OF A 250-BED HOSPITAL

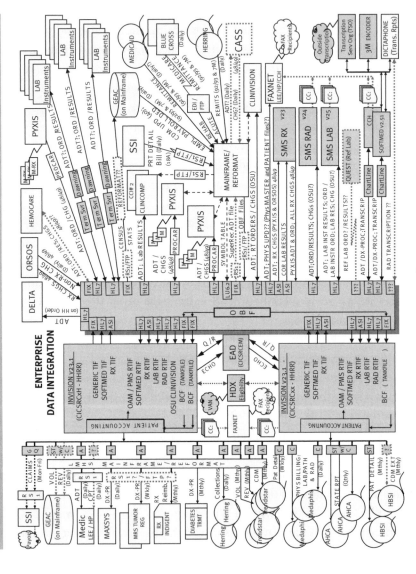

Source: MBA Inc. (www.mbanews.com; copyright 2007).

the risk of losing information and developing inefficiencies, and the general risk of patient care can occur with disconnect of information flow. Unfortunately, ERP planning is a concept that has the least amount of controls. The risk can be a complete system failure with major disruptions to the operations of the enterprise.

The auditor role is often missing during any type of ERP planning or transition. The auditor role appears on the scene after the implementation of the new system. Auditors can play a critical role during the design and prior to the purchase of the new system. They can ask critical questions from an internal control perspective regarding the computer, the software, and the hardware to be utilized. In addition, they can test to see whether the new system will meet all the post-audit information requirements in order to be compliant with any regulatory or industry market expectation.

Numerous e-health system audit considerations are incorporated throughout this book. In addition to developing a comprehensive operational audit checklist, it is important to develop the appropriate *people list*. For example, it is important to develop a multidisciplinary team of users. End-user acceptance and use is critical. However, experience has shown that all possible users are not sufficiently defined. The omission often results in new vulnerabilities and significant cost overruns. For example, at a 500-bed facility, the statistician and financial planners were not included on the front end during discussions of system design and their specific user requirements. Once the new system was up and running, they were scheduled for training.

During the training session, it was quickly realized that tracking information to measure revenue by department was not included in the system design. In essence, the facility lost its ability to monitor various service charges. The statisticians and financial planners should have been included in the review of the new system design. In essence, a questionnaire of all front- and back-end users should be included to ensure that the new system will incorporate the information needs of all users of the system.

How Is Health Information Created?

Health information is the by-product of any and all activities that can occur within a healthcare episode. It is generated by the individuals and entities within the healthcare continuum and is communicated verbally and via paper, facsimile, and electronic avenues.

My previous publication, *Healthcare Fraud Audit & Detection Guidebook*, introduced the market players in the HCC to identify each party's involvement in the provision of direct and indirect patient care. Just as it is critical to understand the movement of financial and health information throughout the continuum to detect waste, fraud, and abuse, this understanding is also important when auditing the content and infrastructure of any e-health system. Exhibit 1.3 reflects the movement of a single health episode through one or more parties.

The parties above the dotted line in Exhibit 1.3 are considered legitimate market players; the illicit market players (white-collar and organized crime) lie below the dotted line. The figurative separation demonstrates that criminals seek opportunities to penetrate the normal flow and movement of a healthcare episode and that fraud can occur within a single market player or as a collusion scheme with one or more parties. Auditors should take into consideration that the market is segmented, fragmented, and at times insulated from other members of the

EXHIBIT 1.3   PRIMARY HEALTHCARE CONTINUUM MARKET PLAYERS

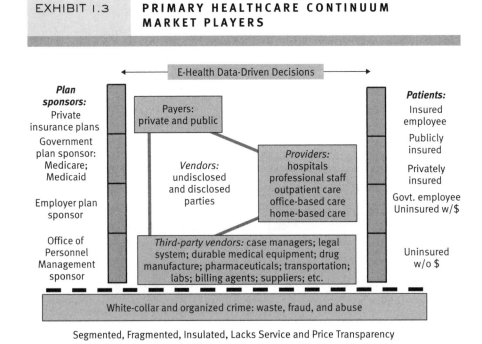

Source: MBA Inc. (www.mbanews.com; copyright 2007).

primary healthcare continuum. With respect to auditing e-health clinical information, it is important to understand the following:

- What e-health information is being generated?
- Why is the information being generated?
- Where is the information being stored?
- Who is using the information?
- How is the information being used?

The integrity of any e-health information infrastructure depends on the ability to answer these clinically related questions.

With respect to auditing e-health financial information that often lacks price (the actual cost) and service (the actual treatment or product) transparency, it is important to understand the following:

- What fees are being generated for the service or product provided?
- Why are the fees structured in the format presented?
- Where are the fees being processed and stored?
- Who is making the financial determinations?
- How are third parties getting paid and what are their fees?

The integrity of any e-health information infrastructure also depends on the ability to answer these financially related questions.

REVIEW OF PRIMARY HCC MARKET PLAYERS

Patients

At the primary level of the healthcare continuum, patients are classified from a financial and clinical perspective. A patient is a party who is a recipient of health services. Within the healthcare continuum, patients are first labeled by their financial status. A patient may be financially classified as an "insured employee," "privately or publicly insured," "uninsured with financial assets," or "uninsured without financial assets." Patient financial status sets the tone for how patients will be handled from day one of a healthcare episode and impacts what offerings other members of the healthcare continuum will make available to them. The effect of a patient's financial status on a healthcare episode will be discussed in further detail in Chapter 3. For now, identifying the concept and discipline of financial case management is enough. *Financial case management* is the discipline of creating a financial plan to meet the patient's healthcare needs. A clinical case management plan focuses only on the healthcare needs of the patient. The market should recognize each discipline as a separate function. From an auditor's perspective, remember to take into consideration the contractual and financial incentives that occur naturally in the marketplace.

From the patient's perspective, the other activity occurring during a healthcare episode is clinical case management (CCM). *Clinical case management* includes current healthcare initiatives and past treatment regimes. It will also be discussed in further detail in Chapter 3. Considerations for an e-health environment should take into account both financial and clinical market activities.

Providers

A provider is any clinical setting and professional staff that designs, implements, and/or executes any healthcare initiative. Healthcare initiatives may be part of a wellness or an illness program, and can be preventive in nature. An initiative may overlap into the secondary healthcare continuum when a patient and provider participate in research-related activities for clinical treatment.

Third-Party Vendors

The category of *third-party vendors* in Exhibit 1.3 consists of a large group of diverse market players. For instance, both durable medical equipment and pharmaceutical vendors fall into this broad category. Third-party vendors also include transportation services that move patients to and from treatment centers. Entities in this category generally support the treatment regimen designated by the provider and carry out necessary supplemental functions in the provision of care by providers.

Payers

A *payer* as illustrated in Exhibit 1.3 is an entity that processes the claims payment transactions of healthcare episodes. Payer systems are also referred to as *third-party administrators* (TPAs). TPAs administer health plan programs on behalf of plan sponsors. A *plan sponsor* in essence is an entity that funds a health program. Exhibit 1.3 illustrates several different types of plan sponsors. Private insurance companies, for example, take a calculated risk by collecting premium payments from a group of individuals. They take the risk that the total amount of premiums collected will be below the cost of healthcare claims paid out. For instance, BCBS associations may sell an insurance plan in which they take the risk. The insurance company will adjudicate the claims based on its insurance plan program. Many insurance companies also act as TPAs and self-administer claims on behalf of other plan sponsors. They sell TPA services in which the self-insured employer takes on the "risk." The role in this example of BCBS would be to process and adjudicate the claims for its self-insured client.

The federal government–sponsored program Medicare contracts out the function of processing and adjudicating claims to a TPA. This TPA processes and adjudicates claims based on program rules on behalf of Medicare's beneficiaries. Another federally sponsored and state-managed benefit plan is Medicaid. Medicaid programs are state run with their own specific program rules. They may contract out the processing and adjudication of claims to a TPA vendor, or some states may process them internally. Patients associated with this type of program are referred to as *recipients*.

The private employer will either purchase an insurance program or choose to provide healthcare benefits to its employees but remain self-insured. In this situation, the employer is choosing to take on the risk. Many employers will hire a TPA to administer their program and process the claims. Again, the idea is that they will be able to keep their costs down. When an employer hires a TPA, it is important to recognize whether the entity is a business entity that functions only as a TPA. The TPA does not sell insurance. This is in contrast to other entities that do have insurance business but also provide TPA services to self-insured employers.

The office of personnel management handles the healthcare benefits for government employees. Just like employers, this office tends to outsource the claims-processing function to a TPA. Therefore, a TPA can have among its clientele private- and public-health-sponsored programs.

Overall, Exhibit 1.3 highlights four typical plan-sponsor profiles. It is important to appreciate that the dynamics are very different. Any audit should take into consideration the contracts between the parties and the respective e-health environment. A clear understanding of what information is exchanged is very important.

Finally, there is the illicit market player categorized as "organized crime." These perpetrators have developed all types of fraudulent schemes in the paper world and have continued in the semi-electronic and paper world of healthcare. As the market moves into the electronic era, expect to evolve new schemes. Internal controls within each legitimate market player will have a critical role in preventing, deterring, and detecting new schemes in the e-health world. The opportunities for effective and rampant schemes are exponential in an electronic environment. However, the opportunities for early detection are just as numerous if careful planning and security are included in any e-health infrastructure. The need to audit controls and appropriate internal guides in e-health requires the development of a second layer of the healthcare continuum. The market players for consideration are referenced in Exhibit 1.3.

REVIEW OF HCC SECONDARY MARKET PLAYERS

Exhibit 1.4 identifies users of health information in roles outside of direct and indirect patient care activity. They may include research, monitoring, and respective public and private agency work.

The secondary HCC includes the global issues of privacy, security, confidentiality, and integrity. The central point is the generation of data intelligence. Several market players impact the generation of data intelligence. Start on the right of Exhibit 1.4 with *public health*, which is the body of science that focuses on the health and well-being of our communities. Public health involves various activities, such as research, education, prevention initiatives, mitigation initiatives, and surveillance of any developments of adverse conditions. The market has numerous organizations, both public and private, dedicated to this science.

The Centers for Disease Control (http://www.cdc.gov), a government-sponsored agency, has as its mission "To promote health and quality of life by preventing and controlling disease, injury, and disability," leading

EXHIBIT 1.4 **SECONDARY HCC MARKET PLAYERS**

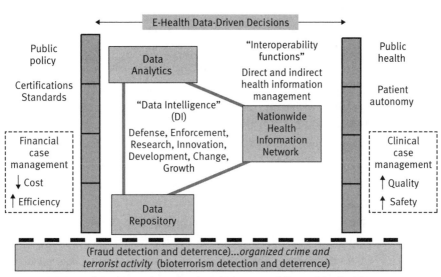

Source: MBA Inc. (www.mbanews.com; Copyright 2007).

with the vision for "Healthy People in a Healthy World—Through Prevention." The key issue of prevention can be maximized with aggregating health information. The ease of processing large amounts of information within a time frame for optimal impact of such information can occur in an electronic environment.

Another example of an organization focused on public health is the American Public Health Association. This organization dates back to 1872 (http://www.apha.org/). The focus of this group is on the health and welfare of communities along with preventing serious threats. The HCC in Exhibit 1.4 continues with the concept, following public health with *patient autonomy.* The healthcare marketplace is faced with many economic as well as data-access issues. The key objective of patient autonomy is to create an environment in which patients have control. This control can occur only if they have access to their own health information. Electronic aggregation of each individual's health records will lay the groundwork for achieving that goal.

The concept of *CCM* is the separation of clinical initiatives and recommendations from any financial aspect of our patients. Clinical case management calls attention to providing independent clinical decision making that is not impacted by any financial factors. This body of science should be developed independently of any financial plan associated with the patient. This leads us to *quality assurance*. This market initiative needs to continue in the form of research, continued studies, data-driven technologies, and monitoring of patient outcomes. *Safety* follows, and is integrated throughout the healthcare continuum. Standards on this subject can be found throughout the marketplace. For example, the Joint Commission (since 1910) on accreditation of hospitals incorporates minimum standards of performance in this area in order for hospitals to receive their accreditation. A more recent organization, the National Patient Safety Foundation, was founded in 1997. Their mission is to improve the safety of patients.

Recent developments in e-health have generated the efforts of the Nationwide Health Information Network (NHIN). This is a Department of Health and Human Services initiative. It has set the following as its goals (http://www.hhs.gov/healthit/healthnetwork/background/):

- Developing capabilities for standards-based, secure data exchange nationally
- Improving the coordination of care information among hospitals, laboratories, physicians' offices, pharmacies, and other providers
- Ensuring appropriate information is available at the time and place of care
- Ensuring that consumers' health information is secure and confidential
- Giving consumers new capabilities for managing and controlling their personal health records as well as providing access to their health information from electronic health records (EHRs) and other sources
- Reducing risks from medical errors and supporting the delivery of appropriate, evidence-based medical care
- Lowering healthcare costs resulting from inefficiencies, medical errors, and incomplete patient information

- Promoting a more effective marketplace, greater competition, and increased choice through accessibility to accurate information on healthcare costs, quality, and outcomes

Any involvement on the subject of e-health should include the monitoring of activities initiated by the Department of Health and Human Services' Health Information Technology initiatives. The Nationwide Health Information Network (NHIH) is setting the stage for an overall data repository from the perspective of the individual patient. The entities within the HCC continuum do have data repositories. However, they tend to be fragmented within their own environment, as illustrated in Exhibit 1.3. Issues of segmentation are found within internal structures and external communications with other entities in both the private and public user marketplace. The future of an interoperable environment will drive data analytics and the generation of data intelligence.

The activities that run parallel on the left side of Exhibit 1.4 begin with *public policy*. Public policy is the set of policies that form the foundation for public law. Much of public policy is generated from the common conscience. For example, the progressive impact of white-collar crime within corporations and the subsequent response of the common conscience initiated public laws such as Sarbanes-Oxley. The HCC continues with *certifications* and *standards*. These activities in e-health specifically are being addressed by initiatives by the Department of Health and Human Services' Health IT activity, as well by numerous other nonprofit professional organizations. Some of these initiatives will be discussed in a later chapter.

Parallel to clinical case management (CCM) is *financial case management* (FCM). In a later chapter, details of this concept will be reviewed further. The market does not formally separate clinical from financial decision making on the management of illness and wellness initiatives. In essence, patients should receive an evaluation from their provider of the most appropriate care (CCM). A separate report and analysis should address the financial picture along with benefit provisions that are available for the treatment options presented (FCM). Separating financial from clinical decisions during the aggregation of health information within any electronic system will provide valuable data-driven opportunities. Most important, it will provide the consumer with clear, independent decision making. This creates an environment in which true patient autonomy and empowerment can exist. The combination of these efforts will decrease cost and increase efficiency, quality, and patient safety. An interoperable e-health environment will promote data intelligence leading toward direct and indirect health information management.

The users in the secondary healthcare continuum along with the primary healthcare continuum have the opportunity to create a truly data-driven market through an interoperable e-health environment. The key component is the data-driven aspects that e-health can provide to these secondary users. Their work product will ultimately feed back into the market players in the primary healthcare continuum. In the primary HCC, data-driven health information models can drive both clinical and financial decision making. The results of these decisions in turn feed into the secondary healthcare continuum. The two forums are contemporaneous as well as reactive and responsive to the respective parties. Exhibit 1.5 provides a sample listing of HCC user activities.

Exhibit 1.6 provides a sample of key questions that should be asked in any e-health environment or among any of the market players involved in the primary or secondary HCC.

Major Initiative for E-Health

The Department of Health and Human Services has been taking steps toward the development of a truly interoperable environment. The key information source to monitor is the "Health Information Technology" home page that can be found at http://www.hhs.gov/healthit/.

In May 2007, the Health Information Technology (Health IT) source indicated several goals for Health IT initiatives. The mandate is to promote comprehensive management of health and medical information and to "secure the exchange between healthcare consumers and providers." Health IT will impact the following areas:

- Improve healthcare quality.
- Prevent medical errors.
- Reduce healthcare costs.
- Increase administrative efficiencies.
- Decrease paperwork.
- Expand access to affordable care.

EXHIBIT 1.5	SAMPLE E-HEALTH PRIMARY AND SECONDARY HCC USER ACTIVITIES

✓ Patients: Individuals who are trying to manage their own health or that of a loved one.

✓ Providers: Professionals and facilities establishing the most appropriate environment and means to serve their patients.

✓ Payers: Providing claims management services.

✓ Employers: Providing healthcare benefits.

✓ Government employees/investigators: Government programs have added significantly to their staffing to address initiatives for creating an electronic environment for all health records and transactions. How to audit in the e-health marketplace will be part of most compliance initiatives, investigations, and enforcement.

✓ Higher education: In response to all types of fraud- and e-health-related issues, upper graduate programs are being developed to provide degrees or certifications in this area. Healthcare is an offering academics are trying to develop as a subspecialty. The e-health network is providing greater sources of research material to develop outcome-data-driven clinical decision-making programs.

✓ Health attorneys have litigation activity throughout the healthcare continuum. Understanding how to audit in the e-health world will impact how cases are litigated and how various subject matters are addressed.

✓ Internal audit groups will be impacted by developing new skill-set offerings in order to audit in a wide range of operational areas, from workers' compensation management to employee health information to the internal controls of drug manufacturers' operational delivery systems of each identified market player.

✓ Fraud examiners will be impacted by e-health environments, and in particular with data-retrieval issues.

✓ Consulting firms will be impacted by significant opportunities for data analytics and data intelligence offerings in the e-health environment.

✓ Provider systems: Case managers' skill-set offerings for auditing e-health.

✓ Payer systems: Case managers' skill-set offerings for collecting e-health information; managing health information as well as auditing their e-health systems.

✓ Employers: Case managers focus workers' compensation on managing e-health issues with information received, maintained, and generated.

✓ Life care planners: Skill-set offerings; considerations for managing e-health information.

EXHIBIT 1.6   **SAMPLE E-HEALTH PRIMARY AND SECONDARY HCC E-HEALTH ISSUE**

- ✓ What is it using the information for?
- ✓ Why is it being used?
- ✓ Where is the information being stored?
- ✓ Who has access to the information?
- ✓ How is it being used?

This initiative targets the concept that interoperable Health IT will improve individual patient care, but it will also bring many public health benefits, including:

- Early detection of infectious disease outbreaks around the country
- Improved tracking of chronic disease management
- Evaluation of healthcare based on value enabled by the collection of de-identified (data that excludes the identity of the patient) price and quality information that can be compared

The primary discussions generated from the inception of Health IT initiatives center around the belief that health information technology is an effective tool to help individuals maintain their health through better management of their health information. The initiatives under this program will help consumers gather all of their health information into one place. This will allow the opportunity to understand its content. This type of control will allow patients to share information securely with their healthcare providers. The ultimate goal is that it will help patients get the care that best fits their individual needs. Overall, the Health IT initiatives will help improve public health. The model is to build partnerships between consumers and providers across the country one relationship at a time.

Audit Implication Overview

This chapter provides a market overview on several separate fronts. First is the introduction of e-information and e-health. Next is a historical overview of technology. Technology goes hand in hand with any discussion of e-information and any e-health framework. Exhibit 1.1 graphically represents the major areas to incorporate when reviewing a particular market player. This is the actual delivery of healthcare products and/or services along with their financial management. Exhibit 1.2 illustrates a sample fragmented data map of one entity. Exhibit 1.4 represents the contract and information world that functions separately and overlaps with the components of Exhibit 1.3. Auditing in e-health is about taking Exhibit 1.1 and identifying the applicable IC dynamics within each market player or within their communication relationships among one or more parties. This exact same concept overlaps into the market players of the Primary Healthcare Continuum (Exhibit 1.3) and the Secondary Healthcare Continuum (Exhibit 1.4). This is vital for the integration of technology into our information continuum. The next chapter continues with concepts of industry applications and their impact on the audit process.

ENDNOTES

1. David L. Sackett, Sharon E. Straus, W. Scott Richardson, William Rosenberg, and R. Brian Haynes, *Evidence-Based Medicine: How to Practice and Teach EBM*, Third Edition (Edinburgh: Churchill Livingstone, 2005).
2. Historical information compiled from the Computer History Museum (http://www.computerhistory.org).
3. Ibid.

CHAPTER 2

Industry Applications

You must be the change you wish to see in the world.

—MAHATMA GANDHI (1869–1948),
PREEMINENT LEADER OF INDIAN NATIONALISM

During the past 100 years, we have witnessed significant advancements in healthcare delivery systems. Today, a true e-health environment has the ability to derive data intelligence on an almost real-time basis and presents unprecedented opportunities to benefit individuals and communities. This chapter discusses industry applications within two frameworks: the users of health information and the evolving market standards and resources. To fully appreciate and audit the users of health information, it is first important to have a process to identify every user. As the market evolves and new standards for building and utilizing e-health systems emerge, auditors will need to include these standards within their audit scope.

Players throughout both the primary healthcare continuum (HCC) and the secondary HCC can use electronic data to their advantage. For example, healthcare professionals can use it to improve clinical care for patients. Health service researchers can use it to better assess quality of service. Government and health service managers can use it to create administrative efficiencies. Health insurers, including Medicare and Medicaid, can use it to prevent fraud and abuse. Public health authorities can use it to improve surveillance and epidemiologic investigations.

To appreciate the intricacy of the healthcare marketplace, consider the list of 30 possible health information uses that might arise during a patient's five-day hospital stay, as shown in Exhibit 2.1.

Auditors need to learn how to identify these and other types of electronic data uses within an e-environment.

Public Uses

Who uses e-health records? What type of system can house e-health records? Will these systems expose patients to any vulnerability? Why can some market players access these systems and others cannot? What patient information

EXHIBIT 2.1	EXAMPLE HEALTH INFORMATION USES DURING A PATIENT'S FIVE-DAY HOSPITAL STAY

1.	Quality assurance	2.	Outcome measurements
3.	Clinical pathways	4.	Cost studies
5.	Protocol development	6.	Case management (including care coordination)
7.	Preparing treatment alternatives	8.	Population-based studies
9.	Health plan performance	10.	Accreditation
11.	Reviewing healthcare professional qualifications	12.	Certification
13.	Evaluating practitioner and provider performance	14.	Licensing
15.	Underwriting	16.	Premium rating
17.	Creation, renewal, or replacement of contract health insurance or health benefits	18.	Ceding, securing, or placing a contract for reinsurance of risk relating to claims for healthcare (including stop-loss insurance and excess-of-loss insurance)
19.	Medical reviews	20.	Legal services
21.	Auditing functions (including waste and fraud and abuse detection)	22.	Compliance
23.	Business planning and development	24.	Cost-management studies
25.	Management and operational planning–related analyses (including formulary development and administration)	26.	Development or improvement of methods of payment or coverage policies
27.	Customer service	28.	Resolution of internal grievances
29.	Due diligence in connection with sale or transfer	30.	Fundraising/marketing activities

is transferring into public domain? (For example, hospitals may be obligated by the state to notify public health agencies of certain contagious diseases.) What are the regulatory requirements that govern transactions?

An auditor's checklist should identify the e-source of all electronic information contained within an e-health environment. Auditors should also identify what internal controls exist or need to be implemented to ensure secure information applications. Finally, auditors should identify each market player's use of electronic information. Exhibit 2.2 offers an audit identification analysis for assessing an e-health environment and identifying its users. The analysis is driven by the primary HCC, and its

EXHIBIT 2.2   **PUBLIC USE ANALYSIS AND E-SOURCE DOCUMENTATION**

Primary Healthcare Continuum (HCC): Clinical, Service, Product, and Financial Integration *Public Use Evaluation*	Public Research	Govt. Reporting	Public Initiatives	E-Source Purpose	Statutory Req't.	Compliance Req't.
Patients:						
Insured employee						
Publicly insured	*Identify applicable roles, functions, and use by the patient within each category of participation or requirement.*					
Privately insured						
Gov't. employee						
Uninsured w/$						
Uninsured w/o $						
Providers:						
Facility type						
Professional staff	*Identify applicable roles, functions, required internal controls, and use by the provider within each category of participation or requirement.*					
Inpatient care						
Outpatient care						
Office-based care						
Home-based care						
Payers:						
TPA w/insurance business						
TPA w/o insurance business	*Identify applicable roles, functions, required internal controls, and use by the payer within each category of participation or requirement.*					
Private plan sponsor contracts						
Government plan sponsor contracts						
Others:						
Case managers						
Drug manufacturers						
Durable medical equipment	*Identify all respective parties, their applicable roles, functions, required internal controls, and use by the various third parties within each category of participation or requirement.*					
Pharmaceuticals						
Transportation						
Legal system						
Labs						
Billing agents						
Suppliers						
Others						
Plan Sponsor:						
Government plan (Medicare and Medicaid)						
Private insurance plan	*Identify applicable roles, functions, required internal controls, and use by the plan sponsor within each category of participation or requirement.*					
Employer-sponsored plan						
Office of Personnel Management						
Organized Crime	*Identify potential third parties and potential sources of breaches.*					

structure ensures the identification of each party impacting the generation and distribution of e-health information.

PRIVATE USES

The primary HCC also functions as the basis for Exhibit 2.3, an auditor's evaluation to identify the use of health information in a private setting. Primary HCC market players use health information in the course of business, delivery of service, or in the receipt of service. Key uses of health information by primary HCC market players include health management, internal control activity, quality assurance, private research, and the actual e-source system.

EXHIBIT 2.3   **PRIVATE USE EVALUATION**

Primary Healthcare Continuum (HCC): Clinical, Service, Product, and Financial Integration *Private Use Evaluation*	Health Management	Internal Controls	QA Research	E-Source System	Minimum Necessary	Privacy Controls
Patients:						
Insured employee Publicly insured Privately insured Gov't. employee Uninsured w/$ Uninsured w/o $	*Identify applicable roles, functions, and use by the patient within each category of participation or requirement.*					
Providers:						
Facility type Professional staff Inpatient care Outpatient care Office-based care Home-based care	*Identify applicable roles, functions, required internal controls, and use by the provider within each category of participation or requirement.*					
Payers:						
TPA w/insurance business TPA w/o insurance business Private plan sponsor contracts Government plan sponsor contracts	*Identify applicable roles, functions, required internal controls, and use by the payer within each category of participation or requirement.*					
Others:						
Case managers Drug manufacturers Durable medical equipment Pharmaceuticals Transportation Legal system Labs Billing agents Suppliers Others	*Identify all respective parties, their applicable roles, functions, required internal controls, and use by the various third parties within each category of participation or requirement.*					
Plan Sponsor:						
Government plan (Medicare and Medicaid) Private insurance plan Employer-sponsored plan Office of Personnel Management	*Identify applicable roles, functions, required internal controls, and use by the plan sponsor within each category of participation or requirement.*					
Organized Crime	*Identify potential third parties and potential sources of breaches.*					

Other concepts important to the assessment of private use of health information are "minimum necessary to execute the task at hand" and *privacy control*. *Minimum necessary* has become a term of art in the world of health information audits that implies that only the minimal amount of information necessary to carry out a task should be reviewed. If, for example, a "biller" pursues payment on an open account, it should not review information from prior accounts that do not directly impact the collection process.

The public and private use tables include organized crime, not to legitimize the activity in any way, but to acknowledge its presence and ongoing efforts to breach e-source systems. Legitimate market players need to address any internal control weaknesses that would allow unauthorized parties to access or use e-health information. Exhibit 2.3 provides more detail on private use evaluation.

As explained in Chapter 1, the secondary HCC addresses the direct and indirect management of health information and its users. Auditors should identify associated privacy issues, e-source systems, required data integrity integration, and relationships and associations impacting each of the primary HCC players. Exhibit 2.4 focuses on the secondary HCC and offers a combined evaluation to identify both private and public use.

EXHIBIT 2.4	SECONDARY HEALTHCARE CONTINUUM PUBLIC AND PRIVATE USE EVALUATION

Secondary Healthcare Continuum (HCC): Privacy, Security, Confidentiality, and Integrity Integration *Private and Public Use Evaluation*	Pubic Use	Private Use	Privacy Security	E- Source System	Integrity Integration	Primary HCC Impact
Access						
Public health			*Identify applicable databases, systems, functions, and their respective collection repositories.*			
Public policy						
Patient autonomy						
Provider autonomy						
Data-Driven Decisions						
Clinical case management						
Financial case management						
Data analytics						
Data Intelligence						
Effective Controls			*Identify applicable roles, functions, and system infrastructure.*			
Certifications						
Standards						
Quality						
Safety						
Cost						
Efficiency						
Interoperability Functions						
Nationwide health information network						
Data repository			*Identify segregated data repositories that function independently.*			
Direct health information management						
Indirect health information management						

INFORMATION CONTINUUM

While the primary HCC identifies direct and indirect healthcare services and the secondary HCC identifies users of health information that result from data gathered during the delivery of direct and indirect healthcare services, the information continuum (IC) consists of the tools that the primary and secondary HCC parties employ to operate within an e-environment. A bona fide analysis of any healthcare environment ideally should address all three continuums contemporaneously. Exhibit 2.5 highlights the key categories and components necessary for a comprehensive review of any entity's IC.

The categories in Exhibit 2.5 continue to develop in the marketplace at different technological rates, and each category requires distinct competencies to understand and appreciate. Auditors should therefore separate their IC review by these categories and ensure that their audit team includes experts for each category.

EXHIBIT 2.5   INFORMATION CONTINUUM

Information Continuum (IC): Segmented, Fragmented, Insulated, Non-par Application and Pace Private and Public Use Evaluation for IC	Primary HCC Secondary HCC Impact	Electronics Market Standards	Computers	E- Source System Networking	Software Languages	Storage
Electronics:						
Devices						
Circuits						
Systems						
Computers:		*Identify current use level of technology by electronic tools, computer use, components, and networking infrastructure.*				
Devices						
Processors						
Level of technology						
Components:		*Identify current use level of technology associated with software languages and storage devices.*				
CPU input/output						
Operating memory						
Storage memory						
Industry:		*Identify applicable roles, functions, and system infrastructure.*				
Regulatory guideline						
Industry specific						
Compliance requirements						
Networking:		*Identify solutions for development tools, standard open interfaces, interoperability, code reduction, scalability, reliability, and security.*				
Network software						
Network system						
Internet, intranets, extranets						
Software Languages:		*Identify current industry standards, regulatory requirements, and compliance guidance standards.*				
Languages controlling operating system						
Languages controlling business operations						
Languages controlling network systems						
Storage:						
Devices						
Data repository systems						
Access and recovery						

Market Standards and Initiatives

A significant amount of legislative and policy activity involving e-health is occurring today. In addition, niche professional organizations have been developing their own standards that may or may not overlap with legislative and policy activity. Monitoring organizations that appear to have an impact on the e-health environment will keep auditors abreast of the latest developments. The list of organizations given here is not meant to be conclusive, but is an assembly of some key players to watch for:

- Agency for Healthcare Research and Quality (AHRQ)
- Health Level Seven (HL7)
- Certification Commission for Healthcare Information Technology (CCHIT)
- Model Requirements Executive Team (MRET) (under the Office of the National Coordinator for Health Information Technology, U.S. Department of Health and Human Services (HHS))
- Association of Records Managers and Administrators (AMRA)
- Department of Defense Records Management Program (DOD Directive 5015.2)

Agency for Healthcare Research and Quality

The Agency for Healthcare Research and Quality (AHRQ) grew out of its predecessor, the Agency for Healthcare Policy and Research (AHPR), when Congress restructured the agency in 1999. The Omnibus Budget Reconciliation Act of 1989 originally formed AHPR as a constituent unit of the Public Health Service (PHS), HHS. Other healthcare research predecessors include:[1]

- PHS's Department of Health, Education, and Welfare (HEW) (1968–1979) and HHS (1979–1989)
- National Center for Health Services Research and Development, Health Services and Mental Health Administration (1968–1973)
- Bureau of Health Services Research, Health Resources Administration (HRA) (1973–1975)
- National Center for Health Services Research, HRA (1975–1978)

- National Center for Health Services Research, Office of the Assistant Secretary for Health (OASH) (1978–1985)
- National Center for Health Services Research and Health Care Technology Assessment, OASH (1985–1989)

Today, AHRQ serves as one of the public health services agencies operating under HHS. Other sister agencies include the National Institutes of Health (NIH), the Centers for Disease Control and Prevention (CDC), the Federal Drug Administration (FDA), and the Health IT initiatives. Leading American universities and institutions act as major sources of funding and technical assistance for health research. They also act as science partners, working with the public and private sectors to build the knowledge base for what works (and does not work) and to translate this knowledge into everyday practice and policymaking.[2] The AHRQ focuses its research efforts for HHS in several areas, including:

- Bio-medics
- Quality improvement and patient safety
- Outcomes and effectiveness of care
- Clinical practice and technology assessment
- Healthcare organization and delivery systems
- Primary care (including preventive services)
- Healthcare costs and sources of payment

Auditors should monitor and incorporate each of these research areas into their e-health information review strategy. In addition, auditors should also pay attention to AHRQ's activities when assessing how a particular e-health environment incorporates research and the most current information at the patient's bedside. Research regarding evidence-based medicine is of particular of importance. In one study, researcher E. Andrew Balas discovered that, on average, it takes as long as 17 years for research to be used in patient care. Balas's study further cited clinical access to the numerous articles as one of the fundamental lags between research and actual implementation. Balas's study prompted a number of further studies by AHRQ designed to improve integration of research directly into healthcare delivery systems.[3] E-health will help narrow that gap between research and implementation. Auditors can trace ongoing agency efforts at www.ahrq.gov.

Auditors should also keep on their radar the Health IT component of AHRQ that aims to help bring healthcare information technology into the twenty-first century. This subgroup of AHRQ has set numerous goals and initiatives pertaining to issues such as the use of technology in day-to-day clinical practice, electronic medical records, privacy initiatives and controls, and infrastructures that will help prevent waste, fraud, and abuse. Auditors can track major market initiatives at healthit.ahrq.gov.[4]

Exhibit 2.6 provides a sample auditor's list of IT topics that will help form the necessary background information required for reviewing an e-health environment. Auditors should evaluate the impact that the primary HCC, secondary HCC, and IC have on each of the key topics identified.

Exhibit 2.7 presents a list of coding systems used in many healthcare information transactions and communications. The significance of each of these coding systems varies. For example, the National Drug Classification (NDC) is the national classification of all drugs registered and approved by the Food and Drug Administration (FDA) and acts as a reference to verify the approval of a particular medication. Another example, the Current Procedural Terminology (CPT) coding system, is used in clinical research

---

EXHIBIT 2.6   KEY TOPICS IN INFORMATION TECHNOLOGY

AHRQ Health IT Key Topics in Information Technology	Primary HCC Secondary HCC Impact	Information Continuum	Electronics Market Standards	E-Source System Networking	Software Languages	Storage
Electronic Standards Enable interoperability by encoding health information using a common language						
Electronic Medical and Health Records Applications						
Computer-Based Clinical Decision Support (CDS)						
Computerized Provider Order Entry Clinical applications						
Telehealth Remote patient monitoring						
Interface Engines Building a clinical-data-sharing effort						
Shared Clinical Data Repositories Development of centralized mechanism for all relevant parties						
Health Information Exchange (HIE) Clinician access and sharing among repositories						
National Council for Prescription Drug Programs (NCPDP) Pharmacy service messenging						
Electronic Prescribing Standards						
Health Level Seven (HL7) Clinical messanging standards						
DICOM Clinical messaging syntax used to exchange medical images						

Auditor considerations in assessment, audit, implementation, or preparation for market initiatives.

EXHIBIT 2.7	**KEY TOPICS IN CODING SYSTEMS**

AHRQ and Other Market Health IT Coding Systems	Primary HCC Secondary HCC Impact	Information Continuum	Electronics Market Standards	E- Source System Networking	Software Languages	Storage
National Drug Codes (NDCs) Standardization of reporting drugs and biomedical products						
Current Procedural Terminology (CPT) Common reporting structure of patient procedures						
Clinical Care Classification System (CCC) Nursing clinical care						
Nursing Interventions Classification (NIC) Reporting structure for nursing intervention						
Home Health Care Classification (HHCC) HHCC of nursing diagnoses and nursing interventions						
The Comprehensive Ambulatory Care Classification System (CACS) National grouping methodology for ambulatory care patients National Ambulatory Care Reporting System (NACRS)						
Logical Observation Identifiers, Names, and Codes (LOINC) Standardization for pooling health information maintained by Rengestrief Insititute						
Systematized Nomenclature of Medicine (SNOMED) SNOMED Clinical Terms (SNOMED CT) Standard Nomenclature of Diseases and Operations (SNDO) College of American Pathologist (CAP's) Standard Nomenclature of Pathology (SNOP) SNOMED International remains a division of the College of American Pathologists (CAP)						
ICD (International Classification of Diseases) International standard for classifying diseases and other health problems (clinical diagnoses) maintainted by World Health Organization (WHO)						
NPI (National Provider Index) National directory of provider identification numbers						

Auditor considerations in assessment, audit, implementation, or preparation for market initiatives.

and has a direct impact on how services are paid for. Each coding system has a particular use in the marketplace and should be considered in the development or analysis of any e-health environment in which the coding system is utilized. Auditors should ensure that they use the most current and applicable coding system. For example, the International Statistical Classification of Diseases and Related Health Problems (ICD) coding system is updated every year.

Exhibit 2.8 presents a sample Health IT architectural overview for an e-health environment.[5] Auditors can use this list as a guideline to ensure that they identify key IT components, including application, communication, process, and devices.

I recently had an opportunity to work on two panels with HHS, which produces ongoing studies, publications, and policy discussion on achieving the optimal Health IT environment, and the Office of the National Coordinator (ONC) for Health IT, which identifies infrastructure issues that leave vulnerability for waste, fraud, and abuse. The ONC also offers recommendations for the development of functional requirements for electronic health records (EHR) that enhance data by reducing the incidence of improper payment and assisting in fraud management.

EXHIBIT 2.8   KEY TOPICS ARCHITECTURE OVERVIEW

AHRQ Health IT Key Topics in Architecture Overview	Primary HCC Secondary HCC Impact	Information Continuum	Electronics Market Standards	E- Source System Networking	Software Languages	Storage

Architecture of Health IT

Application Level
Computerized Provider Order Entry (CPOE)
Clinical Decision Support (CDS)
Electronic Medication Administration Records (eMAR)
Results Reporting
Electronic Documentation and Interface Engines
Electronic Prescribing (E-Prescribing)
Others

Communication Level
Messaging standards: HL&, ADT, NCPDP, X12, DICOM, ASTM
Coding standards: LOINC, ICD-10, CPT, NDC, RxNorm, SNOMED

Auditor considerations in assessment, audit, implementation, or preparation for market initiatives.

Process Level
Health Information Exchange (HIE)
Master Patient Index (MPI)
HIPAA security/privacy
Others

Device Level
Tablet PCs
Application service provider (ASP) models
Personal digital assistants (PDAs)
Bar coding
Others

It has validated its recommendations through public comment and worked extensively with appropriate Health IT organizations to encourage adoption of their recommendations. The final reports that we created can be found at www.hhs.gov/healthit/.

The final report titled "Recommended Requirement for Enhancing Data Quality in Electronic Health Records," prepared for Kathleen H. Fyffe, Senior Advisor, ONC for Health IT, HHS, produced 14 recommended functional requirements to increase EHR-S data accuracy and aid in fraud management:

1. Audit Functions and Features
2. Provider Identification
3. User Access Authorization
4. Documentation Process Issues
5. Evaluation and Management Coding
6. Proxy Authorship
7. Record Modification after Signature
8. Auditor Access to Patient Records
9. EHR Traceability
10. Patient Involvement in Antifraud

AHRQ Health IT Key Topics · Standards and Policy Activity	Primary HCC Secondary HCC Impact	Information Continuum	Electronics Market Standards	E- Source System Networking	Software Languages	Storage
Healthcare Information Technology Standards Panel						
Standards development organizations (SDOs)						
Health IT vendors						
Providers						
Clinicians						
Purchasers						
Payers						
Public health professionals						
Clinical and health services research						
Government agencies						
Consumer organizations						
Health Information Exchange Policy Issues						
"Recommended Requirements for Enhancing Data Quality in						
Electronic Health Records"—June 2007 report						
Numerous reports and ongoing studies						

Auditor considerations in assessment, audit, implementation, or preparation for market initiatives.

11. Patient Identity-Proofing
12. Structured and Coded Data
13. Integrity of EHR Transmission
14. Accurate Linkage of Claims to Clinical Records

Exhibit 2.9 provides a sample listing of current standards and policy activity conducted in the marketplace in an effort to achieve an interoperable healthcare environment.[6]

HEALTH LEVEL SEVEN

To stay current on market activity, auditors should also be aware of Health Level Seven (HL7), an organization founded in 1987 and comprised mostly of volunteers. The American National Standards Institute (ANSI) accredited HL7 as one of several *standards-developing organizations* (SDOs). ANSI, founded in 1918, strives:

> to enhance both the global competitiveness of U.S. business and the U.S. quality of life by promoting and facilitating voluntary consensus standards and conformity assessment systems, and safeguarding their integrity.[7]

HL7 is an information resource for any audit of an e-health environment. *Level 7* refers to the application level—the highest level of the International Organization for Standardization (ISO) communications model for Open Systems Interconnection (OSI). ISO is an international, nongovernmental association providing standards that have been accepted in over 157 countries.[8] In 1982, the ISO identified seven standards levels for networking:

1. Application (Level 7) supports application and end-user processes.
2. Presentation (Level 6) provides independence from differences in data representation (e.g., encryption) by translating from application to network format, and vice versa.
3. Session (Level 5) establishes, manages, and terminates connections between applications.
4. Transport (Level 4) provides transparent transfer of data between end systems, or hosts, and is responsible for end-to-end error recovery and flow control.
5. Network (Level 3) provides switching and routing technologies, creating logical paths, known as virtual circuits, for transmitting data from node to node.
6. Data link (Level 2) encodes and decodes data packets into bits; furnishes transmission protocol, knowledge, and management; and handles errors in the physical layer, flow control, and frame synchronization.
7. Physical (Level 1) conveys the bit stream—electrical impulse, light, or radio signal—through the network at the electrical and mechanical level.

Level 7, the application layer, addresses definitions of the data to be exchanged, the timing of the interchange, and the communication of certain errors to the application. It also supports functions such as security and availability checks, participant identification, exchange mechanism negotiations, and, most important, data exchange structuring.

HL7 implements several initiatives with respect to clinical and administrative data. Three specific e-health standard initiatives and models should be on an auditor's checklist for ongoing review: EHR-S Functional Model (EHR-S FM), the EHR-S Interoperability Model (EHR-S IM), and PHR Functional Model (PHR-S FM). The ANSI-approved EHR-S FM has over 160 recommended functions in specific clinical areas including:

- Direct care functions subgrouped into the following:
  - Care Management
  - Clinical Decision Support
  - Operations Management and Communication

- Supportive functions subgrouped into the following:
  - Clinical Support
  - Measurement, Analysis, Research, and Reports
  - Administrative and Financial
- Informational infrastructure functions subgrouped into the following:
  - Security
  - Health Record Information and Management
  - Registry and Directory Services
  - Standard Terminologies and Terminology Services
  - Standards-Based Interoperability
  - Business Rules Management
  - Information
  - Infrastructure
  - Workflow Management

These categories can be viewed in greater detail at www.hl7.org.[9]

EHR-S IM, also approved by ANSI, focuses on developing characteristics, system, and process requirements in order to achieve an interoperable electronic health record system. In an executive order, President Bush defined *interoperability* as:

> the ability to communicate and exchange data accurately, effectively, securely, and consistently with different information technology systems, software applications, and networks in various settings, and exchange data such that clinical or operational purpose and meaning of the data are preserved and unaltered.[10]

An internal auditor should, at minimum, ensure that an EHR-S environment has appropriate functional and security controls surrounding origination, transmission, and receipt of health information. HL7's website also provides detailed information on the initiatives of this committee, which include:

Section 1: Health(care) Delivery
Section 2: Health(care) Act
Section 3: Act Record
Section 4: Act Record Attributes
Section 5: Health Record

Section 6: Patient Encounter Record
Section 7: Patient Summary Record
Section 8: EHR Interoperability

HL7 announced PHR-S FM in November 2007; it has not yet been approved by ANSI. The model will focus on a system that can stand alone from an EHR system. Model formats will include web-based, provider-based, and employer-based versions, and model frameworks will contain the following three layers:

1. Personal Health:
   • Accountholder profile
   • Managing historical clinical data and current-state data
   • Wellness, preventive medicine, and self-care
   • Managing health education
   • Accountholder decision support
   • Managing encounters with providers
2. Supportive:
   • Provider management
   • Financial management
   • Administrative management
   • Other resources management
3. Information Infrastructure:
   • Health record information management
   • Standards-based interoperability
   • Security
   • Auditable records

Any auditor involved with the development of a PHR should monitor the ongoing developments of this initiative.

CERTIFICATION COMMISSION FOR HEALTHCARE INFORMATION TECHNOLOGY

In 2004, three major organizations combined efforts to form the non-profit Certification Commission for Healthcare Information Technology (CCHIT): American Health Information Management Association (AHIMA), Healthcare Information and Management Systems Society

(HIMSS), and the National Alliance for Health Information Technology (Alliance). Since its inception, CCHIT has received grant funding from HHS for its ongoing development of certification standards and programs for electronic health systems.

CCHIT provides criteria, market standards, and a certification process for electronic health records and their networks. The nonprofit's certification commission workgroups attend to issue areas such as ambulatory, inpatient, network, foundation, interoperability, security, child health, cardiovascular medicine, emergency department, and privacy and compliance, as well as other evolving market issues. It has certification processes in two settings: inpatient and ambulatory.

Ambulatory certification involves the review of three distinct categories: functionality, interoperability, and security. The functionality category consists of numerous criteria segmented into direct care, supportive functions, and information infrastructure capabilities. CCHIT references both HL7 criteria and the Ontario Medical Association's CMS Local Solution Specification V1.3[11] for market standards. The interoperability category is not yet well developed and is limited to certain areas, such as laboratory, imaging, medications, immunizations, clinical documentation, chronic disease management/patient communication, secondary uses of clinical data, administrative and financial data, and clinical trials. The security category includes access control, audit, authentication, documentation, and technical services.

The inpatient certification involves the review of the same distinct categories: functionality, interoperability, and security. Similar to the ambulatory standards, numerous functionality criteria are segmented into direct care, supportive functions, and information infrastructure capabilities. The interoperability category is not as well developed and is limited in focus to information in the inpatient care setting, such as medication, history, and allergy information. However, guidelines discuss certification to include specific testing for orders and administration of medications, and address the discharge or transfer of the patient from the inpatient setting to another healthcare facility, specifying how medication and allergy information will transfer with the patient. Finally, similar to the ambulatory certification, inpatient security categories include access control, audit, authentication, documentation, and technical services.

DEPARTMENT OF DEFENSE RECORDS MANAGEMENT PROGRAM

Introduced in March 2000, DOD Directive 5015.2 details the provisions for implementing the management of records. This standard, unique in structure from the aforementioned, stipulates a minimum functional capacity for the software, interfaces, and search criteria capability of record management. A complete copy of the DOD directive is available online at www.defenselink.mil/webmasters/.[12]

The DOD divides its standards into the following components: six general requirement provisions (C2.1), over 247 detailed requirement provisions (C.2), over 42 nonmandatory feature provisions (C.3), and over 58 management of classified records provisions (C.4).

The general requirements use a straightforward approach to address record management, accommodation of dates and data logic, the implementation of standard data sets, backward compatibility, and accessibility.

The detailed mandatory requirements focus on specific record layout and content as well as scheduling, declaring, and filing records. These requirements also set forth specifics on filing electronic mail messages and storage criteria. In addition, they address vital record management components, such as retention, destruction, cycling, search and retrieval functions, and transfer of information as well as access control requirements. The detailed mandatory requirement section concludes by addressing the database management aspect of the electronic record management system.

The nonmandatory features allow for inclusion of user-specified needs by the acquiring agencies. Examples of user-defined activities listed in the guidelines include management of classified records, storage availability, hardware, and operating system needs.

The detailed nature of these requirements provides a benchmark for any entity considering the development of an e-health infrastructure.

ASSOCIATION OF RECORDS MANAGERS AND ADMINISTRATORS

Established in 1955, the Association of Records Managers and Administrators (AMRA), an international, not-for-profit professional association, is considered an expert in the management of records and information in both paper and electronic form.[13] The organization stipulates professional conduct standards, and AMRA adopts ISO 15489 with respect to record management.

ISO 15489-1 includes standards for records from originating parties, all media formats including hardcopy and electronic, management of created records or records received by any public or private organization during the course of its activities, and activities of individuals who have the responsibility to create or maintain records. It also provides guidance on policy and procedure activities with respect to record policies, procedures, systems, and processes. The standards furthermore integrate guidance regarding quality, design, and implementation of a record system.[14,15]

AUDIT IMPLICATION OVERVIEW

Numerous organizations within the market address e-health issues and provide standards for networking, interoperability, system infrastructure, content, and security. Auditors should identify and fully appreciate all users of information in any environment. E-health auditors should therefore identify users within the primary HCC, secondary HCC, and IC. The exhibits in Chapter 2 provide a checklist approach to ensure the identification of users and tools from a variety of perspectives:

- Primary HCC, including the patient, provider, payer, plan sponsor, and third-party vendors as well as white-collar and organized criminals
- Secondary HCC, including various support roles and users of heath information that do not provide direct or indirect patient care
- IC integrated from a systems perspective

Auditors should not overlook the importance of developing a library of resources for ongoing review of the literature, regulatory front, and technological advances. This chapter introduces several direct healthcare initiatives and resources. It also introduces global perspectives that are not necessarily devoted to healthcare but nonetheless contain expertise regarding the management of electronic information. An auditor's library of resources for e-health, at a minimum, should include ongoing research and studies from the following organizations:

- Agency for Healthcare Research and Quality (AHRQ), www. ahrq.gov

- National Resource Center for Health Information Technology, healthit.ahrq.gov
- Office of the National Coordinator for Health Information Technology (ONC), www.hhs.gov/healthit/
- "Recommended Requirements for Enhancing Data Quality in Electronic Health Records," www.hhs.gov/healthit/
- Health Level Seven (HL7), www.hl7.org
- American National Standards Institute (ANSI), www.ansi.org
- Certification Commission for Healthcare Information Technology (CCHIT), www.cchit.org
- Department of Defense Records Management Program (DOD Directive 5015.2), www.defenselink.mil/webmasters/
- Association of Records Managers and Administrators (AMRA), www.amra.org

E-health continues to develop and transform at a swift pace. Auditors should expect today's environment to be obsolete within the next 10 years. The audit process in e-health requires contemporaneous management of current infrastructure while preparing for ongoing updates and changes to the environment. Auditors therefore should also expect to invest heavily in research in preparation for auditing e-health system infrastructures and resources. The next chapter moves into a discussion of the financial side of e-healthcare—specifically from a case management perspective.

ENDNOTES

1. http://www.archives.gov/research/guide-fed-records/groups/510.html. Records of the Agency for Health Care Policy and Research, U.S. National Archives & Records Administration.
2. *What Is AHRQ?* Agency for Healthcare Research and Quality, Rockville, MD. AHRQ Publication No. 02-0011, February 2002, http://www.ahrq.gov/about/whatis.htm.
3. Carolyn M. Clancy, *AHRQ: A Tradition of Evidence: Federal Agency Carries a Rich History of Involvement in Today's Evidence-Based Medicine Movement—Focusing on the "Evidence" Inside Healthcare IT—Evidence-Based Medicine.* Carolyn M. Clancy, MD, is the director of the Agency for Healthcare Research and Quality, Rockville, MD. *Health Management Technology,* August 2003.
4. http://healthit.ahrq.gov/portal/server.pt?open=512&objID=562&parentname=CommunityPage&parentid=1&mode=2&in_hi_userid=3882&cached=true.

5. http://healthit.ahrq.gov/portal/server.pt?open=514&objID=5554&mode=2& holderDisplayURL=http://prodportallb.ahrq.gov:7087/publishedcontent/ publish/communities/k_o/knowledge_library/key_topics/health_briefing_ 03282006111834/architecture_of_health_it.html.

6. http://healthit.ahrq.gov/portal/server.pt?open=512&objID=653&&PageID= 5664&mode=2&in_hi_userid=3882&cached=true.

7. http://www.ansi.org/about_ansi/overview/overview.aspx?menuid=1.

8. www.iso.org.

9. http://www.hl7.org/ehr/downloads/index_2007.asp.

10. President Bush, August 22, 2006.

11. Copy located at www.ontariomd.ca/cms/infoForVendors.shtml.

12. http://www.defenselink.mil/webmasters/.

13. http://www.arma.org/about/overview/index.cfm.

14. http://www.icrm.org/newsletter/2002fall.pdf.

15. "Electronic Records: A Workbook for Archivists" (ICA Study 16), copyright © International Council on Archives, 60 rue des Francs-Bourgeois, 75003 Paris, France, April 2005.

CHAPTER 3

Impact of E-Health on Case Management

It is not the strongest of the species that survive, nor the most intelligent, but the one most responsive to change.

—CHARLES DARWIN (1809–1882), ENGLISH NATURALIST

The market's response to managing patient care is critical if we are to survive our current healthcare crisis and provide cost-effective quality-driven healthcare. Adapting the discipline of case management to the e-health environment could have an evolutionary impact on healthcare. This chapter discusses traditional case management and introduces the need to subdivide it into two separate orders: *financial case management* (FCM) and *clinical case management* (CCM). In addition, the chapter discusses *informatics* and its integration into case management. An understanding of case management and informatics is important for auditors conducting reviews anywhere within the healthcare continuum.

What is case management? How is it currently applied? What needs to change? *Case management* describes the science behind the multidisciplinary approach to managing the health plan of a patient. CCM, the management of patient health from a clinical perspective, has been in existence in various formats within the healthcare community for some time. FCM, the management of patient health from a financial perspective, is a new and emerging component of patient healthcare management. The Association of Case Managers defines case management as:

> A collaborative process of assessment, planning, facilitation and advocacy for options and services to meet an individual's health needs through communication and available resources to promote quality cost-effective outcomes.[1]

Nurses often find themselves in the role of case manager. The American Nurses Association (ANA) defines nursing as:

> . . . a caring-based practice in which processes of diagnosis and treatment are applied to human experiences of health and illness.[2]

As with other healthcare professionals, the definition and roles of nursing continue to evolve. The original pioneer of nursing, Florence Nightingale, established herself as an accomplished administrator during the Crimean War with insight well beyond her era. Consider two of her famous quotes that date back to 1859:

> It may seem a strange principle to enunciate as the very first requirement in a hospital that it should do the sick no harm.[3]
>
> No man, not even a doctor, ever gives any other definition of what a nurse should be than this—"devoted and obedient." This definition would do just as well for a porter. It might even do for a horse. It would not do for a policeman.[4]

Nightingale's "do the sick no harm" objective holds true today. In fact, the role of a nurse has continued to evolve over the past century and a half. Today, for instance, we recognize nurse practitioners as primary care providers and assign them approved reimbursement codes. The practice of case management is traditionally provided by nurses. Over the past decade, other allied healthcare professionals, such as licensed practical nurses (LPNs) and rehabilitation professionals, have been found in case management roles.

E-health will spawn continued evolution in other areas of healthcare as well. One of these areas is the discipline of informatics. *Informatics*, in its most basic form, is "the study of information processing; computer science."[5] One definition of nursing informatics reads as follows:

> Those collected informational technologies which concern themselves with the patient care decision-making process performed by health care practitioners.[6]

The market, however, has broadened its definitions of informatics as applied to healthcare. The British Medical Informatics Society, for example, supplies the following definition:

> The terms "medical informatics" and "health informatics" have been variously defined, but can be best understood as meaning the understanding, skills and tools that enable the sharing and use of information to deliver healthcare and promote health.
>
> "Health informatics" is now tending to replace the previously commoner term "medical informatics," reflecting a widespread concern to define an information agenda for health services which recognizes the role of citizens as agents in their own care, as well as the major information-handling roles of the non-medical healthcare professions.[7]

It is appropriate here to introduce *infomediary specialists*. The dictionary defines an infomediary as:

> Any company or Web site that gathers information from various sources, [especially] about goods for potential customers; also, a company that gathers information about consumers and markets it to other companies while preserving consumer privacy.[8]

An infomediary specialist, therefore, is a professional dedicated to the gathering of pertinent information. A healthcare infomediary specialist obviously gathers pertinent health information. The adaptation of case management and the integration of informatics in the e-health marketplace will place healthcare infomediary specialists in a position to not only gather and provide information but also provide patient-centric case management services.

As the science of health informatics evolves, it will be important to evaluate its impact on case management. Understanding health informatics, case management, and the infrastructure that delivers this patient service is critical to auditing patient care in an e-health environment.

FINANCIAL PICTURE

Auditors also need to appreciate the management of the financial aspect of clinical services rendered to patients. The marketplace continues to have a significant amount of pressure on it to control the cost of managing a patient's illness. Case managers therefore often find themselves handling both clinical and financial concerns.

When a provider determines an appropriate plan of care for a patient, clinical variables impact the formulation of the plan. But how much of that plan is impacted by financial considerations? When a payer denies the use of a nongeneric cancer treatment and recommends a slightly different generic treatment, is that a financial or clinical decision? When a provider consistently chooses the highest-reimbursed chemotherapy, is that a financially or clinically based decision? When the system limits healthcare professionals from offering treatment regimens due to price, is the patient's welfare compromised? A significant market conflict often exists between clinical and financial concerns.

Case managers currently neither segment nor delineate clinical and financial considerations when communicating treatment plans to patients. Does the provider meet the standard under the Patient Bill of Rights if it does not provide full disclosure on all treatment options without any limitations due to coverage issues? If the patient is presented with only the treatment option approved by the payer, then standards are not being met. What if a patient walks into a provider setting and "buys now" without being informed of all the costs associated with the care ordered? The expectation that the patient receives a treatment plan solely in the best interest of his clinical condition should be a minimum standard. Communication regarding the financing of the plan should nevertheless also be required.

As well as providing greater and quicker access to information, e-health certainly presents the ability to create a more transparent healthcare environment. However, the market must evolve to recognize the distinctions between clinical and financial case management and effectively implement these two separate functions necessary to managing patient care.

HOSPITAL-BASED FCM APPLICATION

FCM based in a hospital setting should ideally contain continual proactive training and educational programs to manage change, mitigate transaction errors, and assure financial integrity in an environment of complex reimbursement requirements. The following case study presents the implementation of my FCM model and its separation from CCM in a hospital setting.

Background Information and Provider Perspective

I first applied my FCM model at a 240-bed community hospital based in Illinois between the years 1992 and 1998. While all direct and indirect providers of patient care focused on their core clinical competency, the hospital separated all financial duties and delegated them to a "charge team" that managed every patient within the hospital from a financial perspective.

Lost revenue due to problems such as payer denials, inappropriate discounts, missed charges, late charges, and write-offs hurts the financial performance of healthcare providers. Complex payer criteria, increased regulations, and an increased workload for clinicians and other personnel responsible for revenue processing contribute to the magnitude of financial challenges that providers face.

In the community hospital, a team originally known as the *Charge Team* removed all financial functions from staff that had direct or indirect patient care activity. This team evolved into a multidisciplinary team, referred to as *Financial Case Managers*, assigned to follow patients from admission to discharge. The team managed the significant revenue components of the accounts receivable pipeline. They primarily prevented or corrected errors in revenue processing at the time of patient service and assured complete, timely reimbursement for patient services provided.

The Financial Case Managers found that a lack of multipayer expertise and full-time employee (FTE) resources devoted to monitoring payers limited provider financial performance. The typical model for providers calls for a focus on selected managed-care or Medicare patients instead of daily management of all payers. Addressing each and every payer proved a key factor to the success of the Financial Case Managers. In other words, the Financial Case Managers operated regardless of the type of insurance the patient carried and even operated when the patient did not carry any insurance. To assure accurate reimbursement, the team's methodology called for staff training on all payer criteria for all types of patients.

The Financial Case Managers realized key benefits. Clinicians could focus more on patient care, leading to improved customer satisfaction. Standardization of revenue processing occurred in all areas of the hospital. Increased flexibility to changing payer requirements improved compliance with payer regulations and contracts, and improved accounting for the cost of patient care also developed. My FCM model is a concurrent, proactive program that separates the financial management of the patient from clinical services to prevent revenue-processing and documentation errors at the time of patient service. It ensures complete and timely reimbursement.

Problem: Getting Paid Correctly for Services Provided

Receiving appropriate reimbursement in an environment of constantly changing reimbursement rules and complex payer requirements can be overwhelming. How does a provider manage its contracted revenue on a day-to-day business? Are the traditional roles of case management and utilization review addressing the payer requirements in a way that assures that providers receive appropriate reimbursement? Where do delays or losses in payer reimbursement come from, and how do we prevent them from occurring?

Exhibit 3.1 illustrates the typical flow of a provider's accounts receivable pipeline from preadmission to final account payment. Highlighted are the potential sources of error at each position in the pipeline that can contribute to denials, delays, or discounts in payer reimbursement.

EXHIBIT 3.1   **TYPICAL PROVIDER ACCOUNTS RECEIVABLE PIPELINE**

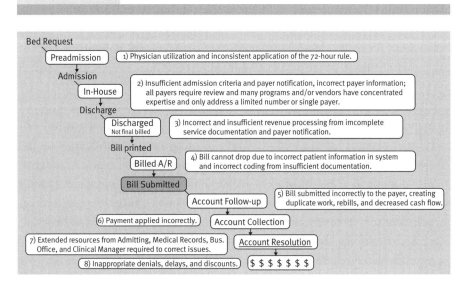

The first potential breakdown occurs at the point of patient entry into the hospital with application of the *72-hour rule*. Medicare requires that any preadmission testing within 72 hours of admission be accounted for and included on the inpatient bill. Failure to do so may subject the hospital to fines. Processing the patient into the hospital with the appropriate admission criteria and payer information and notification therefore is critical. In fact, providers must follow correct verification, authorization, and notification processes throughout the patient stay. The nature of healthcare tends to place a priority on the patient's medical needs and denote the processing of information as secondary. As a result, providers may treat patients with required services but fail to document and process the correct information required to ensure appropriate reimbursement.

While clinical personnel typically perform in-house processing of charges, their intuitive interest typically aligns with the care of the patient. The increase in patient acuity, patient-to-nurse ratio, and the stress of daily activity furthermore demand patient care to take priority over charge and revenue processing. Meanwhile, complexity in the management of multiple-payer criteria, verification-authorization-notification procedures, and carveout exceptions continue to increase. When a provider reconciles patient accounts with the wrong or insufficient information, it will not receive the contracted payments from managed-care contracts and may subject itself to an insurance audit or fines from Medicare. Appropriate documentation of patient services remains imperative to receiving the correct reimbursement and avoiding audit liability. (There is a motto in health accountability: "If it wasn't documented, then it wasn't done!")

When an error occurring in the pipeline is discovered after discharge, a provider may need to rely on the resources of several departments to receive correct reimbursement. For instance, admissions may need to correct status information, medical records may need to make coding adjustments or provide document management, and the business office may need to follow up on accounts and rebill the invoice. The more errors in the pipeline, the more expensive it is to correct a bill and to collect appropriate reimbursement. Inappropriately documented patient services or payer notification cannot be corrected retrospectively. The Financial Case Managers therefore found it more effective and less expensive to *prevent* and correct errors in the pipeline at the time of patient service and before discharge.

Prior to the application of the FCM model, errors regularly occurred at the point of patient access during physician and nursing documentation, because of clinical data, medical record, electronic medical record, and resource management, and due to medical staff and patient accounts. Because a different skilled individual handled each process point, nobody in the pipeline had an understanding of every process point, let alone the knowledge of complex payment criteria and the clinical background to follow patient care. The Financial Case Managers reviewed the same information for reimbursement that is reviewed for quality-of-care issues. Although their tasks were rooted in financial transactions, their clinical training allowed them to recognize care-based issues and pass them onto the clinical case managers immediately.

The Financial Case Managers executed their task according to the following hypothesis: it is cost effective to proactively monitor and correct errors at various process points, at the time of patient service, to ensure that specific payer criteria are met and that there is correct and timely reimbursement.

Findings

Experienced clinical nurses and allied health support staff trained to understand clinical diagnosis and procedures for patient care developed the FCM model. This team also had medical audit experience and understood hospital charge entry procedures, medical record documentation, payer contracts and requirements, and hospital operational systems. While the FCM model primarily operated to assure accurate and complete reimbursement for hospital patient services delivered, other important functions included:

- Proactively monitoring each process point of the accounts receivable pipeline at *the time of patient service* to prevent or correct errors *before discharge*
- Ensuring the correct application of all payer criteria
- Ensuring the application of verification, authorization, and notification
- Facilitating patient understanding of the clinical diagnosis and procedures
- Ensuring complete entry of charges

- Ensuring appropriate medical record documentation to support charges and DRG assignment
- Integrating hospital functions that traditionally did not interact: hospital services (clinical staff) and the business infrastructure (business office and finance)
- Independent, unbiased clinical staff focusing on financial integrity of the hospital
- Reporting transaction errors to appropriate departments (e.g., clinical transaction errors to clinical case managers)

Exhibit 3.2 illustrates how the FCM model integrates into a hospital environment. Integration occurs with business infrastructure, hospital patient services, payer criteria and requirements, and the processing points of patient information to achieve complete and timely reimbursement.

Exhibit 3.3 hightlights the revenue assurance objectives for payers. Providers can benefit by monitoring and preventing errors in each category of the AR pipeline.

The FCM model is intended to be a proactive solution implemented at the time and place of service to monitor, correct, and prevent errors at the processing points of the pipeline. (You could say the model's motto is "Do it right the first time!" at all points of activity—from the moment the patient enters the healthcare system throughout the entire reimbursement cycle.) Exhibit 3.4 provides an overview of the functions associated with the financial management of patients in the provider setting.

EXHIBIT 3.2   FINANCIAL CASE MANAGEMENT INTEGRATION MODEL

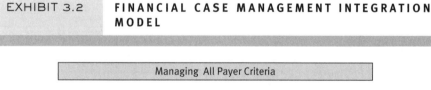
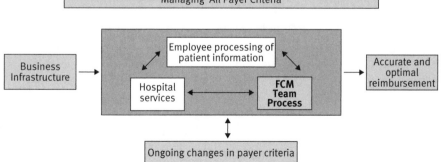

EXHIBIT 3.3	PAYER FINANCIAL CASE MANAGEMENT PROGRAM REVENUE ASSURANCE OBJECTIVES

Medicare:

✓ Appropriate documentation to support a DRG assignment and accurate case mix

✓ Appropriate documentation for accurate observation versus admitting classification

✓ Appropriate discharge or transfer of a patient

Managed Care:

✓ Appropriate application of payer criteria to prevent inappropriate denials, delays, and discounts

✓ Complete charges applied for percentage contracts

✓ Appropriate management of processing carveouts

✓ Appropriate documentation to support any payer audit

Commercial:

✓ Complete charges for complete reimbursement

✓ Appropriate documentation to support the bill in comparison to the record

EXHIBIT 3.4	HIGHLIGHTED FUNCTIONS OF THE FCM PROCESS

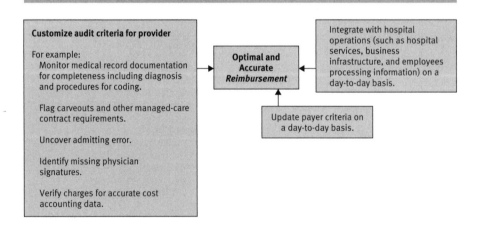

In addition to assuring accurate and timely reimbursement, the FCM model minimizes the accounts receivable buildup that occurs due to incorrect processing. As a result of the Financial Case Managers, the finance department reported improved cash flow. Relieving admissions, medical records, and the business office from having to review and correct processing errors after discharge also increased hospital efficiency.

The FCM model also has an unintended beneficial consequence. Because the Financial Case Managers handle charge entry revenue processing, clinicians have significantly more time to focus on care and can give more attention to their patients. Both clinical staff and patients alike have noticed the impact. Furthermore, the FCM team standardized revenue processing in each of the areas of the hospital it monitored. With a small, specialized team of personnel monitoring the accounts receivable (AR) pipeline and responding to changes in payer criteria, regulations, and contract requirements, implementation became a smoother process. Documentation compliance also became more manageable because the FCM team monitored patient charts during the time of service. Finally, the team's monitoring of charge entry and documentation of patient services improved the availability of information to determine the true cost of patient care.

The Financial Case Manager team's optimal hours of operation were noted on a 12-hour-day, seven-days-per-week schedule. The evening-hour activities were effectively handled during the first 4 hours of the 12-hour workday. The team gradually became integrated into the hospital through the following phases:

- *Assessment phase:* Define management objectives and analyze the scope of the revenue problem. Select the appropriate qualified members for the Financial Case Manager team. Provide the appropriate hospital-based finance training to the team. Place the team in selected areas of the hospital to analyze the AR pipeline and current problems. Analyze previous payer denials, missed charges, late charges, and documentation compliance. Provide a quantitative measurement of selected criteria and current loss of revenue.

- *Trial phase:* Implement the Financial Case Manager team on a trial basis to measure selected criteria, including efficiency of revenue processing and effectiveness in providing complete and timely reimbursement. Compare team results to a baseline formulated from the assessment phase. Conduct and report a comparison analysis.

- *Implementation phase:* Expand the FCM model where successful trials occurred. Continue to measure and report effectiveness on a routine basis. A hospital may choose to outsource Financial Case Manager staff and management to an independent audit firm. Utilizing an independent audit firm further segregates conflict of interest when pursuing the financial integrity of the hospital. Clinical case management objectives can be maintained by the hospital's case management staff.

*   *Retraining phase:* Provide ongoing training in market issues and reimbursement issues and integrate new developments into the FCM model.

Additional Findings

Although the Financial Case Manager team targeted the financial management of the patients treated at the hospital, they also received training in clinical issues to establish a resource for the Clinical Case Managers, who monitor patient care. The team's clinical expertise provided a backup resource to mitigate potential medical errors and/or minimize the impact of a recognized error. See Exhibit 3.5 for an illustration of the clinical services pipeline.

EXHIBIT 3.5   CLINICAL SERVICES PIPELINE CHART

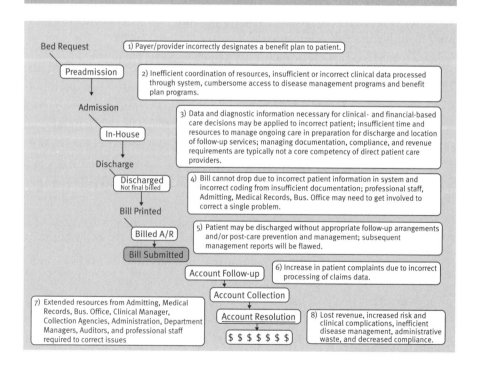

Summary

Hospitals should separate patient FCM from CCM. When separated, the contemporaneous management of financial and clinical issues evolves. The separation of services also removes the conflict of interest that can result when one individual makes both clinical and financial case management decisions. The FCM model creates a medical records–based charge capture and revenue management system. It also greatly reduces charges that post 24 to 48 hours after a patient leaves a facility, thereby eliminating unnecessary follow-up work for the business office. The FCM model ensures that providers capture charges appropriately and continually update their charge master.

Prior to the implementation of the FCM model at the community-based hospital in Illinois, it experienced an average of 40 insurance audits per month. The number of audits fell to less than 4 per year because the model provided a process to ensure contract compliance with both private and public payers. The most significant measurement of success, however, was the hospital's return on investment: for every dollar spent on the FCM program, the hospital generated eight extra dollars.

CONSUMER-BASED FCM APPLICATION

The inability to manage change is the fundamental cause of most (if not all) inefficiencies that exist in healthcare. The consumer or patient perspective of FCM provides a foundation for a consumer to manage market and government changes while engaging in the traditional practice of receiving healthcare goods and services. Tools for managing change do not exist in any e-healthcare program offering. Insurance companies, hospitals, physicians, and patients do not have a resource to predict, manage, or control the cost of an episode of care. Yet, under consumer-directed health plans, all are expected to do so. A consumer FCM application is the missing link that will help place the patient in a position to manage, control, and predict an episode of healthcare.

As the dot-com world continues to generate avenues to manage health information, technology companies try to turn a quick profit with rudimentary static clinical concepts. Tools aimed at helping patients manage their healthcare episodes do not exist. The e-health market has failed to fully execute and/or produce a business offering that facilitates the concept of buying healthcare goods, managing personal health information from a clinical and financial perspective, and managing services in a world with very complex rules. Traditional market and government forces drive these rules. A business model offering that does not integrate these concepts will not survive or, at minimum, will produce ineffective results.

Financial Case Management is needed at the consumer level. Patients in our healthcare system are placed into one or more of the 500,000-plus recognized diagnoses and receive one or more of the 200,000-plus officially established procedures. A hospital may have as many as 10,000 rules to apply to these diagnoses and procedures, and these rules may change monthly, quarterly, and annually.

When a patient enters a hospital or clinic, the doctor or nurse must be ready to assess the patient, select one or more of the diagnosis and procedure codes, and have a cost-effective plan of care ready to execute at any given notice by a government-sponsored program. How are healthcare providers able to do this? The market has provided managed care as its answer. *Managed care* is the arrangement for healthcare in which an organization, such as an HMO, another type of doctor–hospital network, or an insurance company, acts as intermediary between the person seeking care and the physician. It is the system that manages healthcare delivery to control costs. Hospitals expanded the roles and concepts of case management in response to managed care and other payer initiatives.

Case management (our traditional term for all the activities that a physician or other healthcare professional performs to ensure the coordination of required medical services), when coupled with managed care, becomes a comprehensive, labor-intensive process that covers patient evaluation, treatment planning, referral, follow-up, and payment collection. Case management involves strategies defined and developed to facilitate the management and delivery of quality clinical care in a setting of constrained resources. Cost-containment strategies have been integrated into case management. These programs have included critical pathways, clinical maps, clinical trajectories, integrated plans of care, quality controls, and the cost-effective delivery of patient care.

Defined contribution is supposed to replace *managed care*. Instead of having the payer or some other third party drive selection and choice, defined contribution considers the patient a consumer in the center of the selection process. It provides patients the opportunity to specify the care they will receive and control the dollars contributed to their healthcare plan.

Conceptually, defined contribution seems like a worthy endeavor. Practically, however, if providers, insurance companies, and employers had difficulty managing the selection, execution, and cost management of particular diagnoses and procedures, then how do we expect patients to understand the diagnosis and procedure selection process, the treatment choices available, and the complex payment rules necessary to make effective healthcare decisions without FCM tools?

Patient-directed healthcare in e-health presents the opportunity for a *virtual case management system* (VCM). VCM and infomediary specialists will provide patients the resources to select, manage, control, and predict the cost of an episode of healthcare.

MARKET PROBLEMS: THE INDUSTRY AS IT OPERATES TODAY

Patients, providers, employers, and insurance companies face logistical nightmares in effectively managing financially related healthcare information. Effective patient management tools simply do not exist. Opportunities for follow-up care, for instance, often slip pass patients and providers unrecognized. Without effective patient management tools, ongoing governmental and market changes coupled with the intricate healthcare (diagnoses and procedures) selection and maintenance process will continue to cause financial healthcare management to elude our patient-consumers. Patient care also suffers.

Exhibit 3.6 represents a flowchart of how reimbursement is fragmented in the healthcare system. Payers need to manage their benefits by employer rules and providers need to manage their claims by payer rules.

Today, patients must manage their healthcare expenditures using the Explanation of Benefits (EOBs) that they receive from their insurance company after an episode of care. Dave Barry, from the *Washington Post*, captured the utility of an EOB well when he quipped:

> Comically titled Explanation of Benefits, which looks like it was created by the Internal Revenue Service from Hell. It's covered with numbers indicating my in-network, out-of-pocket deductible; my out-of-network, nondeductible pocketable; my semi-pocketed, non-workable, indestructible Donald Duckable, etc. . . . What am I supposed to do with this information?[9]

EXHIBIT 3.6   **FRAGMENTATION BETWEEN THE PAYER AND THE PROVIDER**

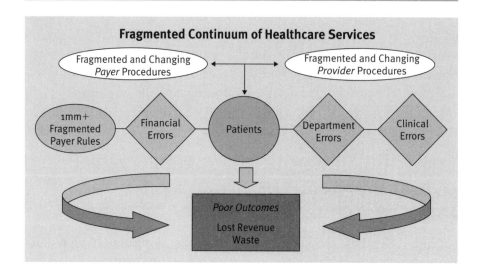

Fragmented Continuum of Healthcare Services

A VCM e-health model that recognizes and separates the financial (FCM) and clinical (CCM) management of patient care will help all parties (in particular, patients) manage health information and episodes of care.

CONSUMER FCM MODEL

In 1996, I began introducing patients to a specific FCM structure, which I referred to as *Healthcare Portfolio*, to facilitate the personal management of their health. I have since developed Healthcare Portfolio into an electronic personal health record (e-PHR) offering that I call PortFolia[sm]. An introductory section of Healthcare Portfolio explains the concept of self-management to patients and provides instructions on:

- What a Healthcare Portfolio is
- Why patients need a Healthcare Portfolio
- What goes into a Healthcare Portfolio

- How to get started on a Healthcare Portfolio
- How to take care of a Healthcare Portfolio

The Personal Health History prepares patients to formulate their personal historical health information. It also includes a complete medical history questionnaire and provides instructions on how to:

- Request medical records
- Authorize release of health information

The Personal Health Financial Management helps patients manage their financial health information. It provides instructions to help patients request financial documents from providers and health insurance companies such as:

- Claim histories from payers
- EOBs from payers
- Correspondence with payers
- Billing statements from health providers
- Health Savings Account (HSA) or other employer-sponsored health account activity

Healthcare Portfolio also includes a Buyer Beware section that educates patients to manage vulnerabilities and avoid being victims of fraud. It includes where to get up-to-date fraud alerts regarding providers, payers, suppliers, pharmaceuticals, and supplements.

The complexity of the healthcare environment also calls for patients to be prepared from a legal perspective. The legal section of Healthcare Portfolio provides support pertaining to:

- Powers of attorney
- Living wills
- Articles and research documents
- Background information on providers
- Healthcare associations
- Support groups, charitable organizations, and research organizations

Paperwork can often overwhelm patients. Even the most well-intentioned personal health record infrastructures or tools often lack a resource to smooth out the bumps in the road. With this understanding, I decided to utilize nurses trained in finance, case management, medical audit, and fraud to offer infomediary instruction, assistance, research, advocacy, and support services for patients. I call these trained professionals *health infomediary specialists* (HISs).

I also include a collection of general forms in Healthcare Portfolio pertaining to:

- Emergency contacts
- Provider contacts
- Insurance information
- Fingerprint identification
- Hair sample
- Personal health goals
- Medical history:

    Personal health assessment
    Personal health timeline

- Current personal health:

    Allergies
    Drug allergies
    Asthma
    Immunizations

- Active illness management
- Illness history:

    General
    Surgeries
    Hospitalizations
    Serious illness

- Future surgeries
- Active wellness management:

    Skin
    Respiratory
    Cardiovascular
    Gastrointestinal
    Neck

Head–ear–nose–throat
Eye
Hematological
Musculoskeletal
Neuropsychiatric
Dental
Endocrinological
Gynecological

- Family tree
- Family history
- Travel history
- Religious requirements
- Work history and work environments
- Military service records

Because many healthcare issues involve pharmaceuticals, such as the coordination of care from multiple prescribing providers, the potential for medical errors, the cost associated with these medications, and medication management by the patient, the Healthcare Portfolio also devotes a separate section to pharmaceuticals that includes:

- Market overview of current issues
- Current medication status
- Medications and supplements history

Other sections Healthcare Portfolio provides to help patients manage their healthcare episodes relate to:

- Provider history
- Provider communications
- Announcements and informational materials (sorted by specialty)
- Second opinions and opinions of payers
- Records collected by facility or surgical center
- Records collected by doctor or specialist
- Records collected of all medications
- Preparing for doctor visits (including question log)
- Planning ahead

These sections may also be used as an auditor checklist to evaluate any personal health record (PHR) management system.

HEALTHCARE PORTFOLIO APPLICATION

The following case studies demonstrate how Healthcare Portfolio assisted three patients who were stuck in the healthcare system. The first case exemplifies the ideal use of Healthcare Portfolio, in which it prepares and empowers patients prior to the occurrence of any adverse event. The second and most common case shows how Healthcare Portfolio helps to mitigate an issue after its occurrence and highlights the role of the health infomediary specialist as an independent advocate and resource. The third case illustrates the concurrent use of Healthcare Portfolio and a health infomediary specialist during receipt of a service.

CASE STUDY #1 HEALTHCARE PORTFOLIO IMPLEMENTATION *PRIOR* TO ADVERSE EVENT

I met "Dina," a 56-year-old female diagnosed with cancer in 2001, and encouraged her to apply the FCM/CCM process by implementing the steps outlined above in the Healthcare Portfolio. I followed Dina for several years.

Prior to receiving any cancer treatment services, Dina encountered seven different licensed professionals who each directed a portion of the assessment for her initial treatment. As she traveled between each provider, Dina realized that not one of them had a complete record of her care that incorporated information from each of her other six providers. Each provider therefore planned to make his or her assessment without complete information from Dina's other concurrent providers. Uncomfortable with this scenario, Dina began to accumulate and share her own record of information from and with each provider as she traveled between them.

Dina eventually made the decision on an initial course of action to treat her breast cancer. It involved a breast lumpectomy, and she was given anesthesia for the first time in her life. Dina then underwent the very unfortunate experience of intraoperative awakening. Although she woke up in pain, crying in the recovery room, her physician at the time told her that "she was just dreaming."

As Dina continued her course of treatment, the anesthesia incident became part of her own traveling Healthcare Portfolio.

During subsequent surgeries, Dina asked the anesthesiologist to review the operative record from her breast lumpectomy. The doctors thanked her for preventing further medical errors, and she never experienced intraoperative awakening again.

In year three of her cancer treatment, Dina received her first denial from her insurance company. This was a healthcare access issue that involved payment denial of services ordered by her provider. Because of Dina's initial investment in FCM organization, she had all the necessary information at her disposal to advocate for herself in any correspondence with her insurance carrier and was able to mitigate the presenting issue. Specifically she was able to provide the "medically necessary" documentation that justified continued treatment.

The combination of FCM and CCM helped Dina make a cohesive and comprehensive initial treatment option. CCM also helped discover an unknown allergic reaction to anesthesia that resulted in one episode of intraoperative awakening and prevented future medical errors by empowering Dina to share the discovery with subsequent providers. Finally, through FCM, Dina had the information to address the financial matters impacting her ongoing care.

CASE STUDY #2   HEALTHCARE PORTFOLIO IMPLEMENTATION *AFTER* ADVERSE EVENT WITH HIS SUPPORT

"Kevin" was about two and a half years old when I met him and his parents. He had experienced ear infections and undergone subsequent procedures since birth. Due to the nature of the ear infections, Kevin was not progressing in his motor development and his desire to crawl and be mobile was resulting in atrophy of his muscles and stunted development. Kevin's doctor ordered physical therapy, but the insurance carrier denied the treatment on the basis that developmental delay was not a covered item and that the issue was not medically related. Due to the severity of atrophy, Kevin's parents initiated his physical therapy treatment out-of-pocket. During this time, they also continued to pay Kevin's insurance premiums for his policy, which they purchased independently as small business owners.

Kevin's parents came to me with their predicament, and I advised them to retroactively implement Healthcare Portfolio's FCM and CCM processes from the time of Kevin's birth. The clinical data collected demonstrated that Kevin's condition indeed resulted from medical problems associated with his ear infections.

Kevin's parents also collected two years of correspondence with the insurance carrier and brought them to me. Acting as their Health Infomediary Specialist, I noted that these letters lacked specific correspondence language that ensures patient rights under the Patient Bill of Rights.[10] Patients have a *right to information*. "Patients own a right to receive accurate, easily understood information to assist them in making informed decisions about their health plans, facilities and professionals."[11] I also determined that Kevin's insurance plan was subject to the State of Illinois Department of Insurance and wrote a letter on behalf of the patient to the private carrier.

Although the next correspondence also resulted in a continued denial of service, the denial finally included information on the patient's right to appeal to the Department of Insurance. I then proceeded to submit Kevin's appeal to the state. Several weeks later, Kevin's parents received a letter from the state noting that the carrier reversed the denial and confirming payment to the hospital. Finally, I helped Kevin's parents reclaim their original out-of-pocket expenses.

Kevin's parents received the requisite instruction to manage health information through FCM and CCM; education and training under the Patient Bill of Rights; advocacy support pertaining to appeal rights with the Department of Insurance; and support while obtaining a refund from the hospital for paying covered expenses out of pocket.

CASE STUDY #3   CONCURRENT IMPLEMENTATION OF HEALTHCARE PORTFOLIO AND HIS SUPPORT

"Laura" was a 36-year-old mother of two. When the time came for Laura to be admitted into the hospital for a medical (not fertility-related) hysterectomy procedure, she already had established a relationship with me. I visited Laura in the hospital on the first day following surgery and initiated both the FCM and CCM processes.

During this initial visit, I noticed that Laura (now sans uterus) was receiving intravenous Pitocin—a medication often utilized to induce labor. When an evening-shift nurse entered the room, I questioned the purpose of the medication. Before leaving the room, the evening-shift nurse replied "She is not getting Pitocin . . . the drug is just mislabeled."

Eight hours later, Laura was still on Pitocin and began complaining of severe migraine headaches. When the day-shift nurse came in, she apologized to Laura and promptly removed the Pitocin, replacing it with normal saline. The day-shift nurse explained that she had been working a 12-hour shift and must have inadvertently hung the Pitocin instead of implementing the standing routine orders.

Frightened and unaware of what complications might result from the nurse's error, Laura turned to a professional she knew and could trust. She turned to me—her health infomediary specialist—as a professional who would put her own interests first and who could advocate on her behalf. After contacting the drug manufacturer, I found that specific research on the impact of Pitocin on women without a uterus did not exist.

Ever since surgery, Laura had continued to experience adverse issues with her bladder. (Although she never filed a medical malpractice claim, the hospital never submitted a bill for the surgery.)

As Laura's HIS, my CCM support services mitigated the damages of an active medical error and were a resource for Laura's clinical questions not sufficiently answered by her provider. I continue to support Laura to this day and have helped her through three other errors relating to this hysterectomy surgery. FCM services were provided in obtaining approval from the payer for subsequent care related to the postoperative complications.

VIRTUAL CASE MANAGEMENT

Virtual case management (VCM) is case management where the communication of information and provision of services function in a true state of interoperability. A VCM e-health model that recognizes and separates FCM and

CCM will help all parties (in particular, patients) manage health information and episodes of care. VCM will automate the decision-making process, facilitate recommendations, and communicate personalized information and advice. It will create the infrastructure desperately needed to manage healthcare services in a defined-contribution or managed-care environment. E-health-environment auditors will need to test to ensure that VCM tools empower patients, encourage access, can mitigate errors, and provide patients with ability to advocate for themselves. The ideal model for VCM in the e-health environment will vary depending on the market player at hand.

VCM Payer Model

The VCM *payer model* addresses the management of patient-requested services, the fees associated with those services, and ensuring appropriate capture of all associated payment criteria. For example, a request for a hip replacement typically involves either a telephonic, facsimile, mail, or electronic submission from a provider. A service request could also be directly submitted by a patient. Payer service request responses therefore involve labor-intensive manual processes. They are dependent on specific users such as review staff or claims adjustors to interpret payment criteria, which can result in inconsistent application of those criteria. In addition, the staff may not effectively separate financially based decisions (e.g., denying service because it is not covered by the patient's plan) from clinically based decisions (e.g., denying service because it is not medically necessary). A VCM payer model should recognize and separate the concepts of CCM and FCM to gather data intelligence about how their decisions are made to better serve the insured and reduce risk resulting from inappropriate claims handling.

Payers find themselves in the uncomfortable position of preventing conflicts of interest from occurring when making decisions on coverage. Conflicts arise when denying a patient a service causes an insurance company a direct financial gain. Payers therefore will constantly wrestle with well-defined processes that protect the insured from receiving medically unnecessary services versus those that thwart costly medically necessary services. Payers must also bear the burden of continuously screening claims to catch false claim submissions. Unfortunately, the screening can compromise legitimate patients with legitimate diagnoses who are being treated by legitimate providers.

VCM Patient Model

A VCM *patient model* will support a new healthcare environment where patients acting like customers will drive the treatment selection process using an intelligent electronic web-based application equipped with tools for comparative analysis and interactive decision making. These tools will engage patients and will, over time, learn to address patient needs and concerns.

The VCM patient model should allow patients to manage the selection and management of services within and out of network. The VCM patient model should address CCM, FCM, and the other issues covered by Healthcare Portfolio. Although numerous vendor offerings promote personal health management record systems, self-directed patient case management tools do not exist. Today's PHRs still fail to prevent patients from falling through the cracks of our healthcare system or to support those already stuck. Therefore, I have upgraded Healthcare Portfolio into PortFolia^sm, a patient-centric, Internet-based personal health record management application, and integrated Health Infomediary Support service support into its design. I designed PortFolia^sm, Medical Business Associates' electronic personal healthcare record offering, to help patients take control of their healthcare experience.

VCM Hospital Model

I provided the FCM *hospital model* in the community-hospital case study earlier in this chapter. That case study demonstrates how the separation of FCM and CCM causes significant improvements in efficiency while patients are in the hospital. Separating FCM from CCM also improves efficiency after patient discharge by enabling hospitals to better manage future services and reimbursement issues. When a hospital performs hip-replacement surgery on a patient, for example, it may miss the opportunity to provide rehabilitation services to the patient upon discharge. Hospitals have various case management methodologies for inpatient monitoring, but managing postoperative care and general subsequent care can be a logistical nightmare. Managing outpatient care is currently a manual, disconnected process where individuals must make phone calls and depend on laborious facsimile transmissions on a case-by-case basis to place patients. Automated post-discharge case management tools do not yet exist in the marketplace.

VCM Physician Model

A VCM *physician model* should allow physicians to better manage future services and reimbursement issues once they determine a patient's diagnosis and treatment plan. The separation of CCM and FCM, with a trained physician and an informed patient, will help both parties in organizing, structuring, and advocating active and future care.

For example, when a physician diagnoses a patient with a severe arthritic condition of the hip and recommends a total hip replacement, the physician cannot proceed with his plan of care without the coordination of the other players in the marketplace. A payer might decide that it will pay for only 3 days of rehabilitation, but the physician plan of care might require 7 days of rehabilitation for optimal outcome. As a result, a physician could place surgery on hold until completion of the entire plan of care. When physicians recommend a plan of care, they should present the patient with two separate plans: a CCM plan defined by the prescribed regimen and an FCM plan that explains the current financial obligations, determinations, and implications. When patients have this information, they can then make informed decisions when considering their treatment plan. Because patients would know the financial issues that might be in dispute with their insurance carrier, they would be able to initiate an appeal with their carrier based on the two separate plans of care.

The current problem in the marketplace lies in the convoluting of clinical decisions with financial determinations. The patient has a right to both sets of information and assurance that one set of criteria does not impact the other. The VCM physician model provides coordination of approved services and options to facilitate the financing of noncovered services.

VCM Allied Health Services

The market focuses heavily on services provided by physicians and by hospitals. However, the delivery of patient care involves numerous other services. *Allied health services* providers such as physical therapists, dialysis technicians, and other nontraditional professionals will also benefit from a VCM model. For example, when a patient has a total hip replacement, insurance coverage may allow for in-home physical therapy. The VCM allied health services model will enable these types of providers to better manage services and reimbursement issues.

VCM Nontraditional Health Services Model

The science behind many of the benefits of nontraditional provider care services has been around for well over a hundred years, if not longer, but due to limitations of payer coverage, patients typically finance these services directly. Nontraditional services providers therefore have a leg up in the marketplace because, unlike traditional providers, they are not dependent on payers for their revenues. A VCM *nontraditional health services model* will nevertheless enable better management of services and reimbursement issues in this segment of the market. When a patient has a total hip replacement, for example, policy coverage may provide for some type of limited chiropractic rehabilitation services or acupuncture for pain management. The VCM nontraditional health services model will help integrate the information generated by the nontraditional providers with that of traditional care providers, whose services are typically recognized by the payer community.

VCM Other Business Services Model

With the advent of e-health, it is important to recognize other types of related services in the marketplace. For instance, healthcare infomediary specialists facilitate management of patient services, ensure policy requirements, and resolve reimbursement issues. Other business providers could include disease management firms that provide supplemental information to any one of the market players, or a nursing home that temporarily discharges a patient to a hospital for a total hip replacement. Upon patient discharge, the nursing home does not currently have the capacity to directly manage any rehabilitation process. The logistics of finding interim care and lodging for this patient are therefore manual, cumbersome, and limited. Another business provider may include a school system that manages the health records of the children within its school district. The VCM *other business services model* would simplify and automate these processes. Integrating these services into FCM and CCM will promote a comprehensive, effective patient-driven e-health environment.

AUDIT IMPLICATION OVERVIEW

Clinical decisions should be made independently of financial decisions. Auditors should provide reasonable assurance that the current procedures do not allow financially driven conflicts of interest to affect clinical decisions. Separating FCM from CCM in the VCM model will set the stage for developing conflict-of-interest controls throughout the healthcare continuum.

ENDNOTES

1. http://www.cmsa.org/ABOUTUS/DefinitionofCaseManagement/tabid/104/Default.aspx 12/7/07.
2. "Nursing, Health, and the Environment" (1995), http://www.nap.edu/openbook/030905298x/html, copyright 1995/2000, National Academy of Sciences, all rights reserved.
3. Jone Johnson Lewis, "Florence Nightingale Quotes," About Women's History, http://womenshistory.about.com/cs/quotes/qu_nightingale.htm, accessed 12/7/07.
4. Ibid.
5. Informatics (n.d.). *Dictionary.com Unabridged (v 1.1),* retrieved December 11, 2007, from Dictionary.com website: http://dictionary.reference.com/browse/informatics.
6. Staggers, PhD, RN, FAAN, Nancy and Thompson, PhD, RN, Cheryl Bagley, "The Evolution of Definitions for Nursing Informatics: A Critical Analysis and Revised Definition," *J. Am. Med. Inform. Assoc.* May–June 2002; 9(3): 255–261, doi: 10.1197/jamia.M0946, copyright © 2002, American Medical Informatics Association.
7. University of Iowa Health Informatics, © 2005, University of Iowa, http://www2.uiowa.edu/hinfo/academics/what_is_hi.html, accessed December 11, 2007.
8. Infomediary (n.d.). *Webster's New Millennium™ Dictionary of English, Preview Edition (v 0.9.7),* retrieved December 11, 2007, from Dictionary.com website: http://dictionary.reference.com/browse/infomediary.
9. October 2000.
10. http://www.hhs.gov/news/press/1999pres/990412.html, the Patients' Bill of Rights under Medicare and Medicaid.
11. Ibid.

CHAPTER 4

Data in an E-Health Environment

We must all obey the great law of change. It is the most powerful law of nature.

—EDMUND BURKE (1729–1797), BRITISH POLITICAL WRITER

What is *data*? At first glance, this may seem like a simple question with a simple answer. Words such as *information, captured results, statistics, numbers,* and *records* may come to mind. In the context of e-health, consider data as defined and undefined information. *Defined data* is information that has an assigned meaning or significance. *Undefined information*, therefore, is data that appears without an assigned meaning or significance. Both defined and undefined information generates new discoveries and understanding. A comprehensive understanding of data and its purpose provides the framework for auditing any e-infrastructure or exchanges between infrastructures. A well-defined data dictionary is therefore crucial to the success of e-health audits.

The Institute of Internal Auditors provides the following definition of *internal audit*:

> Internal auditing is an independent, objective assurance and consulting activity designed to add value and improve an organization's operations. It helps an organization accomplish its objectives by bringing a systematic, disciplined approach to evaluate and improve the effectiveness of risk management, control, and governance processes.[1]

From an audit perspective, analysis of e-health data can provide reasonable assurance that the e-infrastructure in which the data is received, processed, and contained has sufficient internal control from every operational perspective. Consider the following explanation of *internal control* and its relation to information systems provided by the U.S. Office of Budget and Management:

> Internal Control—organization, policies, and procedures—are tools to help program and financial managers achieve results and safeguard the integrity of their programs. . . . Control activities include policies, procedures and mechanisms in place to help ensure that [objectives are met]. Several examples include: proper segregation of duties (separate personnel with authority to authorize a transaction, process the transaction, and review the transaction); physical controls over assets (limited access to inventories or equipment); proper authorization; and appropriate documentation and access to that documentation.
>
> Internal control also needs to be in place over information systems—general and application control. General control applies to all information systems such as the mainframe, network and end-user environments, and includes [security program] planning, management, control over data center operations, system software acquisition and maintenance. Application control should be designed to ensure that transactions are properly authorized and processed accurately and that the data is valid and complete. Controls should be established at an application's interfaces to verify inputs and outputs, such as edit checks. General and application control over information systems are interrelated, both are needed to ensure complete and accurate information processing. Due to the rapid changes in information technology, controls must also adjust to remain effective.[2]

Auditors therefore should ask several questions when reviewing an e-health system, such as:

- What types of controls are in place to collect and manage all of the relevant forms of health information created during the course of patient care?
- What types of tests can be conducted to ensure a breach of data has not or will not occur?
- Does the system have adequate controls to prevent inappropriate data use?

Today, a variety of market initiatives among recognized industry leaders are formulating market standards for managing e-health information. (Several of these organizations were discussed in Chapter 2.) Because no one specific source for market standards exists, staying informed requires vigilant monitoring of evolving standards. As new e-health system requirements and market standards evolve, e-health information infrastructures will need to implement new controls.

This chapter focuses on understanding the concept of data and provides data audit guidelines for behaviors and activities associated with data. Auditing e-health data begins with setting up a data library of all the information to be reviewed.

DATA LIBRARY

The *data library* consists of the activities that structure the collection and organization of any new or existing data infrastructure. Regardless of where an audit occurs within the e-health continuum, auditors must identify all the data elements used by the particular e-infrastructure under review. Exhibit 4.1 illustrates the flow of data activities that will help identify and document all relevant data components.

The first task of an e-health audit is to identify the subject matter of interest and any impacting factors within the e-environment. Once identification of data in electronic format and data in nonelectronic format occurs, then each data element needs a label and a definition. The following example illustrates the process of identifying one small operational component involved in the processing of a service claim.

Facilities such as clinics and hospitals submit their claims electronically on a form referred to as a UB-04 (universal billing from the year-2004 format). This form contains up to 86 potential elements of data, each defined by the universal billing committee. A provider might record only a portion of these 86 potential data elements. Those elements captured by a provider arrive at a third-party administrator (TPA) or insurance company via the UB-04. The TPA then decides which of the submitted provider data elements they will decide to keep for processing. An employer plan sponsor may receive even less data because a TPA may unilaterally choose not to store certain data elements. Determining why a market player has dropped a particular data element can be important in the identification of any internal control weaknesses.

EXHIBIT 4.1 **AUDIT DATA ACTIVITIES CHECKLIST**

Data Library	Checklist
	audit
	existence
	identification
	definition
	use
	source
	value
	partition
	map
	testing
	redefine
	mine
	modeling
	output
	response
	action
	implementation
	next response
	consequence
	solutions

In the paper world, the original claim document (UB-04) passes through the claims process without any disturbance in content. In e-health, however, market players alter the retention of data elements on electronic claims for various business reasons. Identifying alterations in content or by omission is one of the key functions of an audit impacting the reasonable assurance of data.

Once auditors label and define each data element, they then must note the data element's specific use and delineate multiple uses when appropriate. If a data element's definition does not reflect its use, then the auditor must expand the definition. In defining the source of each data element, auditors must include all prior transitions of the data. If auditors download healthcare claims from insurance companies on behalf of employers, then they should note the appropriate data transactions, which may look similar to the following chain:

(1) Provider *to* (2) Company ABC clearing house *to* (3) Insurance Company DEF *to* (4) PPO Network GHI *to* (5) Insurance Company DEF

to (6 and 7) Vendor Check and EOB Printing *to* Insurance Company
DEF *to* (8) Insured *to* (9) Employer Plan Sponsor *to* (10) Insurance
Company DEF

Data values are not limited to monetary considerations. Data also includes
values that characterize process flow, contractual, and operational issues.

In 2002, I received my first opportunity to audit a brand-new facility that allegedly operated in a completely interoperable e-environment.
The facility was a new, state-of-the-art specialty hospital and my first stop
was in the Emergency Room. Data processing in the ER began with the
registration of the patient and included a few other data movements, such
as the documentation of services provided. I first discovered a problem
with the e-environment when trying to electronically walk the patient to
the Intensive Care Unit (ICU). I found that the e-system lacked the virtual ability to discharge patients from the ER and admit them electronically to the ICU. Instead, the ER handed a paper document to the ICU
nurse, who then input the patient information into the virtual system to
electronically admit the patient into the unit. Auditors must recognize and
understand these types of missing links in e-health environments.

The facility inadvertently limited virtual interoperability between the
ER and the ICU. The team that built the e-environment evidently did
not anticipate or identify all potential data users. They created a road-
block in interoperability by making decisions without an understanding
of all data uses. Auditors should create data maps to determine both virtual and manual data uses and test the map by applying it to operational
data processes. If the facility had tested the electronic movement of a
patient from the ER to another location with a data map, then it would
have identified a breach in interoperability prior to opening.

As an interesting aside, during my course of engagement, I learned that
physician investors had built the facility. At no point in time had these
physicians considered including a morgue in their plans, and they were
caught off guard when they experienced their first adverse outcome of
a patient. A data-map test would have captured this electronic disruption in the movement of data. Once auditors discover missing data, they
should subsequently add the necessary data fields to the data library and
then redefine the process.

The data library in an e-health infrastructure enables the activity of
mining for information. To illustrate, consider the concept of *matter* studied

by scientists. Traditionally, *matter* means *mass that occupies space.* I view electronic data to be equivalent to *mass* in the physical world in that it occupies space within an e-infrastructure.

Scientists recently began exploring the concept of *black matter.* Black matter is all the mass in the universe that people cannot see. Scientists currently believe that most matter in the universe is black matter. Consider e-health as an opportunity to efficiently find and discern black-matter data. E-environments can generate data intelligence by processing previously unattainable information for the healthcare community to use and analyze. In other words, e-health presents the opportunity to shed light on virtual black-matter data.

Mining data elements to generate intelligence is the greatest value proposition in the e-health environment. Creating a well-structured data library will provide opportunities for the understanding and application of data not previously within the reach of the healthcare community. Significant implications of increased data intelligence include the ability to reduce cost, increase quality of care, and thwart the ethically challenged from thriving in a segmented marketplace. Data mining based on a solid electronic infrastructure of defined data elements opens the door to derive intelligence from large amounts of quality information and comprehensive analytical data models.

DATA INTELLIGENCE

When I practiced as a nurse, one of the hospitals I worked at developed a data model for infection rates. We noted a high rate of post-bypass patients on my unit and gradually discerned a pattern revealing that one surgeon in particular had an unusually high postoperative infection rate. The hospital initiated a study that collected and evaluated data from particular medical records. Each medical record required a manual review followed by a manual compilation of findings, additional testing, and, finally, a conclusion. It took a whole year to identify that the surgeon carried the infection and passed it on to his patients during surgery.

E-health environments have the capability to enable the healthcare community to collect, process, understand, and respond to data in an instant. E-health will promote data output that the community can reasonably rely on, but, in some cases, data output may produce inconclusive information. When inconclusive data outputs occur, the proper response is to redefine the prior steps or perhaps reevaluate the original premise or presenting issue.

Once armed with the information necessary to address the unusually high postoperative infection rates, the hospital could implement a response. It removed the surgeon's surgical privileges pending treatment of his infection. The hospital could have also responded by including the development of better monitoring of etiology for postoperative infections or evaluation of employee and staff health policies.

The concept of collecting outcomes by provider now exists, but measuring outcome by specific staff members has yet to reach the marketplace. In an e-health information environment, decision makers can assimilate and process data in a more efficient and timely manner. The virtual world provides the opportunity to analyze outcomes and production at each measurable level and to introduce new data into the healthcare community.

New Data

Data, whether in electronic or manual form, is constantly evolving to meet increased demands for speed, accessibility, and comprehension. Auditors must keep in mind that although increasing the speed at which information arrives can help deliver optimal results, it can also cause hazardous results at an alarming rate. In a hospital setting, the speed of receiving, processing, and reacting to an abnormal laboratory test can generate an adverse outcome to the patient. In the payer world, if 1,000 fraudulent claims are processed per minute, then money can be long gone before an error is realized. Exhibit 4.2 highlights some of the data management concepts involved in the processing of new data.

As new data develops from a data library, results may fall into neural networks. *Neural networks* help identify hidden patterns that are not normally seen with unstructured and undefined data. They help auditors understand the reasoning behind any predictive or deductive model analysis. Neural networks provide specific information that can be broken down into clusters. Clusters in turn can be broken down further into neurons. Neurons therefore necessarily are derived from original data elements. This data directs the transmission of an intermediate response to

EXHIBIT 4.2   **NEW DATA MANAGEMENT PROCESSING CONCEPT CHECKLIST**

New Data	Checklist
	neural network
	hidden patterns
	deductive
	predictive
	information

the information. This process is cyclical: data output leads to the center point of data components, a further breakdown of the elements, and finally the development of a data algorithm. For example, in the provider setting, a neural network may consist of the elements that cause a specific medical error. Any relevant processed data can be used to prevent this error from happening again.

In the payer setting, a neural network may consist of the elements that cause a certain type of fraud scheme. Processed data can therefore be used to produce recognizable characteristics of a fraud scheme for a payer to check for prior to paying a claim. A very simple algorithm to detect fraud could involve a neural network with a list of providers with suspended licenses. A payer handling a claim submitted by a provider with a suspended license would receive an intermediate response to suspend any further action on the claim. The center point would involve the generation of an exception or error report that demands additional intervention and investigation.

Prior to the implementation of HIPAA's administrative simplification mandate, which called on providers to submit claims electronically in a specified format, claims were generally submitted manually. Therefore, during that time, standardized claims submission did not exist, and processors handled each of the $1.5 trillion worth of claims manually. Just imagine the associated transaction costs.

Today's efficiency creates the opportunity to process claims at a rate of thousands per minute. However, the improvement does not come without consequence. Because both legitimate and false claims are now processed at this rate, there is increased opportunity for the ethically challenged to capitalize. Auditors need to ensure a complete understanding

EXHIBIT 4.3   MORE NEW DATA CHECKLIST

	Checklist
More New Data	
	output
	analysis

of all electronic data in an e-environment to define the unethical uses of data and recognize potential areas for breach.

MORE NEW DATA

The ongoing generation of new data generates even more data outputs and presents even more opportunity for data analysis. (See Exhibit 4.3.) E-health opens new doors to detect fraud through effective use of data and its management. The payer claim system provides a simple example of data analytics at work against fraud. For instance, data output may indicate that a particular provider, say, Dr. Speedy, has increased his home visit patient volume from 6 per day to 25 per day. Basic data analysis should recognize 25 patient home visits in one day as an anomaly.

Another physician, Dr. Pull, may see a reasonable volume of patients per day but extract an average of 135 teeth per patient. By profiling Dr. Pull's patients, data analysis should identify 135 teeth pulled per patient as an anomaly (considering that an adult has only 32 teeth).

New data can also improve the quality of healthcare delivery. By measuring and documenting adverse outcomes to medications, for example, providers can make adjustments to treatment protocols.

PROCESSED DATA

The generation of an anomaly is the result of analyzing processed data. *Processed data*, as illustrated in Exhibit 4.4, develops new clusters, neurons, and subsequent etiologies.

Etiology provides the cause and effect of certain sets of data elements. By segmenting clusters by subject matter, neurons acting as the decision tree for processing data elements derive intelligence and lead toward understanding the etiology of anomalies. For example, the etiology of

EXHIBIT 4.4   PROCESSED DATA CHECKLIST

	Checklist
Processed Data	clustering
	neurons
	etiology

EXHIBIT 4.5   CATEGORIES OF DATA ACTIVITY CHECKLIST

	Checklist
Data Warehouse	outputs
	center points
	components
	elements
	algorithm

Dr. Speedy could be that he now has an assistant providing service under his license, or that he completely fabricates the additional visits.

DATA WAREHOUSE

The previous data activities lead us to the *data warehouse*, the final category for handling data. A data warehouse is the home of information that has been gathered and is to be gathered. Without such a warehouse, we would have a black hole of meaningless, unusable information.

Exhibit 4.5 lists the categories of data activity that result from previous data activities and are captured in a data warehouse.

AUDIT IMPLICATION OVERVIEW

From an audit perspective, electronic data and its use in defined algorithms ascends to data-driven, intelligence-based internal control. Integrating internal control into the data-testing process allows for reasonable assurance of data integrity in the financial, operational, and service sectors of e-healthcare environments. This chapter's explanation of data behaviors and elements provides auditors with the necessary checklists to review data within the e-infrastructure of any player within the HCC.

ENDNOTES

1. http://www.theiia.org/guidance/standards-and-practices/professional-practices-framework/definition-of-internal-auditing/.
2. http://www.whitehouse.gov/OMB/circulars/a123/a123_rev.html.

CHAPTER 5

Algorithms

By nature man hates change; seldom will he quit his old home till it has actually fallen around his ears.

—THOMAS CARLYLE (1795–1881), BRITISH HISTORIAN AND ESSAYIST

BACKGROUND

An *algorithm* is a constructed set of specific defined procedures that executes a defined-data-driven set of analytics typically represented in a specified sequence by symbols and numbers. An algorithm answers a specific question in response to a hypothesis or to generate intelligence to create a hypothesis for further analysis. The word *algorithm* in itself has a very long history. The etymology of the word is noted as follows:

> 1699, from Fr. *algorithme* refashioned (under mistaken connection with Gk. *arithmos* "number") from O.Fr. *algorisme* "the Arabic numeral system," from M.L. *algorismus,* a mangled transliteration of Arabic *al-Khwarizmi* "native of Khwarazm," surname of the mathematician whose works introduced sophisticated mathematics to the West (see algebra). The earlier form in M.E. was *algorism* (c.1230), from O.Fr. Modern use of *algorithmic* to describe symbolic rules or language is from 1881.[1]

Algebra, an art and science of relationships, serves as the foundation of the relationship building necessary for the development of algorithms. The father of algebra, Muhammad ibn Mūsā al-Khwārizmī, born in 780, was a Persian Islamic mathematician, astronomer, astrologer, and geographer.[2] Al-Khwārizmī utilized symbols such as letters and numbers to represent the dynamics of these relationships in a book entitled *On Calculation with Hindu Numbers*.

Algorithms would not exist without the basic concept of numbers. The use of numbers dates back to about 300 B.C. by Hindu mathematicians and began with the numeric symbols *1* to *9*. The mathematicians would use a narrative to combine two numbers (e.g., "1 sata 9" equaled the number 19) and eventually invented the numeric symbol *0* to represent emptiness. When the Arab empire invaded India circa A.D. 700, a knowledge transfer occurred, causing significant advancements in all areas of life.[3] The Hindus' mathematical concepts gradually replaced the use of the abacus developed and used by the Greeks and Romans. Fortunately, we are not writing algorithms today with roman numerals!

The next major development in algebra occurred through the work of Fibonacci sometime in 1202. Fibonacci (Leonardo Pisano), known for studying the mating habits of rabbits, observed during the course of a year that each month, each pair produced another pair that would start breeding at two months. He discovered that a pair of rabbits would produce a total of 233 pairs during the course of the year. He noticed the following pattern reflecting the total number of pairs of rabbits at the end of each month: 1, 2, 3, 5, 8, 13, 21, 34, 55, 89, 144, and 233. This pattern, the formula for the Fibonacci ratio, tell us that "the ratio of the smaller part to the larger part equals the ratio of the large part to the whole," and has catalyzed human abstract thought.[4] Fibonacci and subsequent mathematicians applied the concept of calculating a solution to developing models of probability to help us detect and predict behavior.

UNDERSTANDING ALGORITHMS

Algorithms can execute a process or build models for predictive behavioral analysis. An algorithm could be an informal set of processes or a formal, specifically defined process. Formal processes are required for algorithms managed via the use of a computer programming language that tells the computer what to do. One simple algorithm written for an insurance company's claims adjudication system requires that, for every claim submitted, a patient be a member of the company's insurance program. If the patient is not part of that program, then the algorithm directs the insurance company to deny the claim.

An informal algorithm can be expressed using language. Language coupled with the structure of grammar and use of known references can create a prescribed set of procedures. Parties can then communicate procedures to one another in the form of verbal or written communications. Consider the following narrative:

> At approximately 8 A.M. the students will arrive at school to register for the final examination. The test will begin at 9 A.M. Late arrivals will not be allowed into the examination room.

The relationships in the narrative are straightforward. The students, the school, the exam room, the final examination, and a set of time sequences comprise the data elements within the relationships. The order of activity is communicated in written form in linear fashion (i.e., students arrive around 8 A.M. to register for a 9 A.M. test; if students are late, then they face the adverse outcome of being excluded from writing the exam).

Flowcharts are often used to illustrate both informal and formal algorithms. A simple algorithm for the use of an automobile's oil light that notifies drivers when their vehicle is at risk of corrosion from friction may graphically look like the diagram in Exhibit 5.1.

Regular oil changes to reduce friction will promote oil oxidation and reduce deposit formation. Automobile manufacturers therefore equip

EXHIBIT 5.1   AUTOMOBILE OIL LIGHT SIMPLE ALGORITHM FLOWCHART

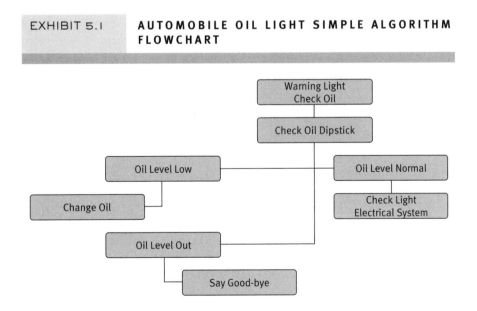

their vehicles with warning lights to remind drivers to change their oil and recommend a set of responses once the warning light illuminates.

Exhibit 5.1 presents three possible scenarios and the elements and relationships involved in responding to the CHECK OIL warning light. Once the CHECK OIL warning illuminates, drivers should check the oil level in their vehicle with a dipstick. If the oil level is low, then drivers should change their oil. If the oil level is normal, then drivers should check to see whether there is a problem with the light's electrical system. If the oil level is out, then driver has a problem! The CHECK OIL warning light may have been an attempt by the automotive industry to create an idiot-proof set of controls to optimize the maintenance of their vehicles by notifying drivers to change their oil within recommended intervals.[5]

We could also create separate flowcharts to follow other considerations that explain why a check oil light is lit in a vehicle. One flowchart might include steps to identify electrical problems with the warning signal. We can then classify groups of algorithms that are similar in scope. In this case, we could create a group of algorithms associated with warning signals in an automobile.

We can also group algorithms into categories defined by how a process is executed. Consider the simple task of logging on to a domain. Exhibit 5.2 provides a simple flowchart of this process.

Users could experience several different scenarios. When a user enters her login and password, the domain reconciles this information with the master database of users. If the user enters correct information, then the domain allows the user to enter. If the user inadvertently enters incorrect information, then the domain denies entry and typically provides the user another opportunity to enter correct information. If the user fails to enter correct information again, then the domain could deactivate the central user profile to ensure that only authorized users enter the domain until further mitigation by the system administrator occurs.

We can also group algorithms into categories to solve a problem. Managing patients at the time of registration often causes a problem for hospitals. A hospital must complete a series of tasks to ensure it gathers correct patient information. If it records incorrect information, then the hospital may jeopardize receipt of reimbursement for services performed. Classifying an algorithm by scope is important for efficiency and effectiveness because different algorithms addressing the same problem may confirm a solution or generate new ones.

EXHIBIT 5.2   **SAMPLE ALGORITHM TO EXECUTE
A PROCESS**

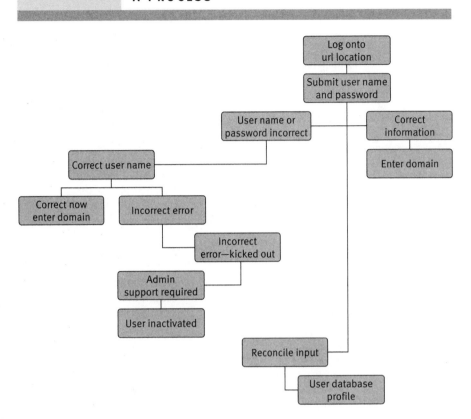

DATA ELEMENTS

Chapter 4 explained the components and concepts behind data elements and provided an auditor's checklist for data behaviors as a framework to identify and organize data. Individual or groups of data elements and the meaning and relationships assigned to them construct every algorithm. Exhibit 5.3 presents an overview of data element behaviors.

In Exhibit 5.3, data use and management activities are partitioned into five sorts: data library, new data, more new data, processed data, and data warehouse. Data library activities organize information to set up particular e-health workflow processes. New data, more new data, and processed data involve ongoing data activities, and data warehouse activity aggregates information for specific applied processes.

EXHIBIT 5.3   DATA ELEMENT BEHAVIORS

Data Library	Checklist	Activity
	audit	determine scope
	existence	document information
	identification	label each activity
	definition	define the activity
	use	define the uses
	source	define route of source
	value	define (nonmonetary) & monetary
	partition	define segmentation
	map	define route of all
	testing	confirm understanding
	redefine	make adjustments
	mine	determine intelligence
	modeling	confirm understanding
	output	measure values
	response	test values
	action	measure outcomes
	implementation	define procedures
	next response	reevaluate infrastructure
	consequence	measure adverse outcomes
	solutions	redefine scope
New Data	**Checklist**	**Activity**
	neural network	subject matter segmentation
	hidden patterns	data processing
	deductive	output intelligence
	predictive	output intelligence
	information	new audit scope
More New Data	**Checklist**	**Activity**
	output	measure values
	analysis	information
Processed Data	**Checklist**	**Activity**
	clustering	information segments
	neurons	information details
	etiology	information intelligence
Data Warehouse	**Checklist**	**Activity**
	outputs	measure values
	center points	benchmarks
	components	dataflow
	elements	data dictionary
	algorithm	data methodology

Contemporaneously developing and managing a data warehouse typically relies on the execution of defined algorithms. Furthermore, the healthcare system's ability to truly reach a state of efficient electronic interoperability depends on how effectively algorithms are programmed. The following case study illustrates how algorithms employ data in an e-health environment.

CASE STUDY

A 400-bed hospital was experiencing an extraordinary high volume of claims denials due to the incorrect receipt and processing of patient admission information by registration staff. While some of this problem could be attributed to patients providing incomplete and incorrect information and staff not following proper procedures, the amount of time and labor required for registration staff to properly interview patients played a considerable role. The hospital depended on adequately trained staff to enter complete and accurate patient information at the time of admission, and the impact resulting from incomplete and inaccurate information was causing significant adverse financial results.

To understand the dynamics associated with this process requires a data library of information. A detailed assessment of the hospital's data library led me to the understanding needed to recommend changes to improve the current electronic transactions and develop new electronic transaction models to minimize the amount of direct labor associated with the registration process. Data testing occurred by capturing new data and more new data, and evaluating processed data.

Studying the dataflow for the task of registering a patient into a facility generated the following patterns:

- Follow-up admission into the facility
- Inpatient rollover admission
- ER walk-in visits
- Outpatient admission for services
- Patient-without-insurance admissions
- Role of financial counselors
- Role of insurance verification
- Role of financial arrangements
- Role of condition of admissions—documentation requirements

EXHIBIT 5.4   DATAFLOW FOR FOLLOW-UP VISIT ADMISSION

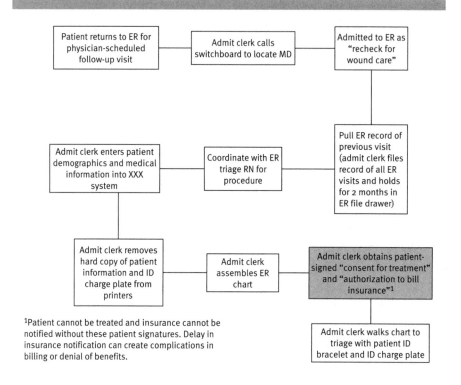

[1]Patient cannot be treated and insurance cannot be notified without these patient signatures. Delay in insurance notification can create complications in billing or denial of benefits.

- Known obstacles
- Role of financial counselors

The flowcharts in Exhibits 5.4 through 5.12 demonstrate the (sometimes complex) patient registration process, functions, and obstacles at different points of entry into a hospital.

The follow-up admission process involved 10 operational functions performed by different types of hospital staff and 2 electronic systems that did not communicate directly. The shaded box in Exhibit 5.4 highlights the fact that patients cannot be treated and insurance companies cannot be notified without appropriate patient signatures and that a delay in insurance notification often creates complications in billing or a denial of benefits.

EXHIBIT 5.5   **DATAFLOW FOR INPATIENT ROLLOVER ADMISSION**

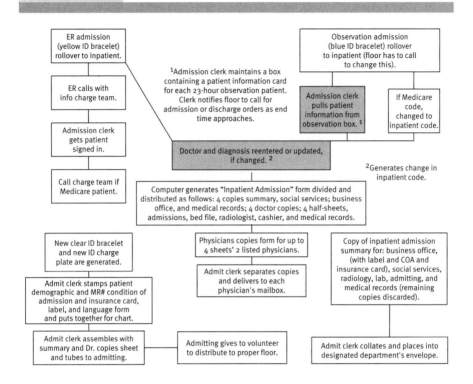

The rollover admission process involved 17 operational components. Any errors in the process can impede the financial integrity of that episode. The two shaded areas in Exhibit 5.5 represent specific data actions that, if omitted or incorrectly processed, result in denial of payment for the entire service episode.

The emergency room admission process also involved 17 independent operational functions. (See Exhibit 5.6.) Any breakdown of information can also lead to lost revenue by the facility. Critical revenue functions are denoted in the shaded boxes.

The outpatient services admission involved 16 different data processes. Each is labor intensive and requires human interaction with paper documents and electronic entry. (See Exhibit 5.7.)

EXHIBIT 5.6   DATAFLOW FOR ER ADMISSION

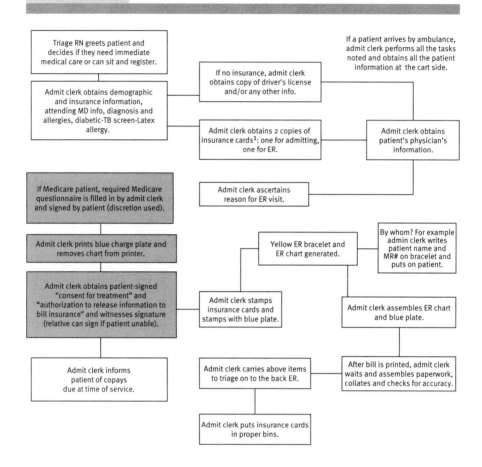

The dataflow shown in Exhibit 5.8 clearly demonstrates that the admission of a patient without coverage was the least invasive mode of entry for the hospital.

Exhibits 5.4 through 5.12 show dataflows that are required to develop a comprehensive data library reflecting the patient registration process. The collection of processed data, new data, and more new data facilitates the menu of data ingredients that feed new algorithms for the processing of these work functions. As processes become digitized, associated data elements will feed the data warehouse.

This hospital had five different avenues for which it could admit a patient into its facility. In total, patient registration involved 66 distinct operational

EXHIBIT 5.7   DATAFLOW FOR OUTPATIENT SERVICES ADMISSION

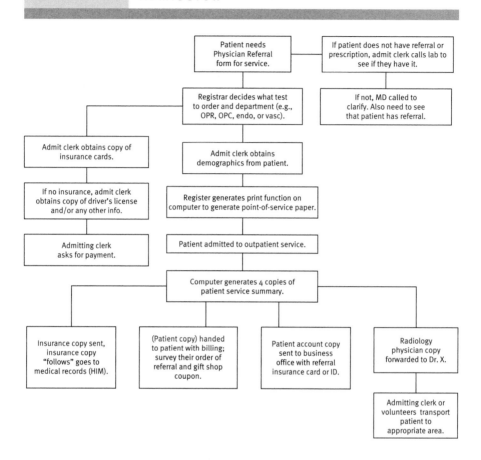

functions and 23 support functions that required manual interaction and were not electronic. Therefore, before the patient even received any services, the hospital flowchart of people and systems involved 89 operational functions (and 4 likely obstacles identified in Exhibit 5.11).

Exhibit 5.13 highlights sample activities that helped identify all the relevant information to develop the hospital's data warehouse. The exhibit lists the audit activities that should be included when evaluating the registration process of a patient. These activities contain algorithms to manage, review, and change processes.

Once patients were admitted, they received service. Exhibit 5.14 illustrates the accounts receivable pipeline for the hospital and provides the key

EXHIBIT 5.8 **DATAFLOW FOR ADMISSION OF PATIENTS WITHOUT HEALTH INSURANCE**

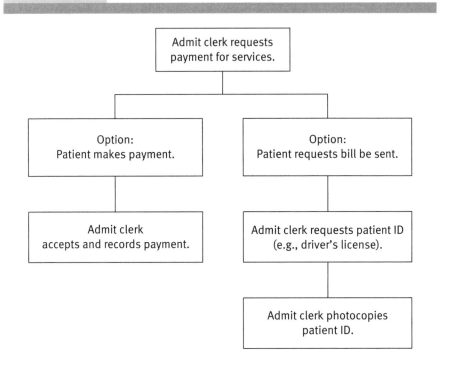

operational components that typically mark patient movement through a facility. Accounts receivable data analysis should proceed throughout the entire business cycle of a hospital.

When auditing an e-health environment, the first step is to create a flowchart from an internal control perspective identifying how one process leads to the next. The second step is to examine how the e-health system electronically communicates with external parties. Professional organizations (described in Chapter 2) initiated market standards detailing how these electronic communications should occur. For example, it is very common that hospitals continuously communicate with payers. One example of an external communication between hospitals and payers involves the certification of patient stay with an insurance company. Exhibit 5.15 illustrates a payer's accounts receivable pipeline.

EXHIBIT 5.9 **DATAFLOW OF OTHER REGISTRATION FUNCTIONS**

Financial Counselors

❑ Responsible for prompt bill drop.

Medicare

❑ Check Medicare and Medicare days for all Medicare inpatients.
❑ Check for Skilled Nursing Benefits (whether or not admitted to TLC; rationale unclear; large volume of work; possibly to assist UR case managers).
❑ Enter patient information into Admission Screening Advisor computer for verification of status.

Insurance

❑ Insurance verification and precertification for all observations, same-day surgery, and inpatients.
❑ Notification of patients scheduled for surgery through Reg Doc printer (self-pay is priority).
❑ Notify UR and insurance companies when an HMO patient is "out of plan" (patients usually transferred when stable).

Financial

❑ Work self-pay accounts, setting up payment arrangements.
❑ Set up payment schedules before elective procedures or surgery.
❑ Handle collection work for copays, deductibles, electives, self-pay, and cosmetic surgeries.
❑ Handle referrals to obtain public aid for eligible patients through outsource corporation.
❑ Verify coding on inpatients so bills drop (check for code specific to insurance, and make sure code noted on chart).
❑ Do case-by-case verifications for billing on clinical screen of SMS.
❑ Quote prices for maternity procedures and/or tests.

EXHIBIT 5.10   **DATAFLOW OF ADDITIONAL PATIENT REGISTRATION FUNCTIONS**

Condition of Admission Forms

❏ Verify that all patients have signed "condition of admission" forms.

❏ Without patient signature, hospital has no authorization to contact insurance for precertification.

❏ Admitting staff notifies counselors when patients who entered unresponsive are able to sign. Counselors go to patient bedside to obtain these signatures.

❏ Signature is required to obtain diagnosis and receive benefits.

❏ Form must be completed in order to forward patient information to the Billing Office; enter patient billing information and insurance contact name and phone number on financial screens.

EXHIBIT 5.11   **DATAFLOW OBSTACLES**

❏ Frequently have to make several insurance phone calls per patient folder, at least one to verify precertification and one to verify benefits.

❏ Insurance cards:
   1. Patients do not carry them.
   2. Cards are outdated.
   3. Patients lose or misplace their cards.
      (Counselors have learned to keep track of insurance information themselves, on their own Rolodex, to speed up verification process.)

❏ Frequently called upon to handle patients' insurance entanglements.

❏ Frequently called by home care to provide patient benefit information and insurance-contact-person information from counselor's screen.

EXHIBIT 5.12   **DATAFLOW FOR FINANCIAL COUNSELORS**

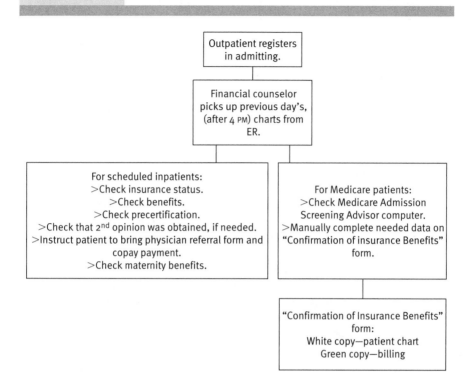

Exhibit 5.15 represents typical operational movement of information and activity. During patient registration, a provider works with claims agents for precertification of services and verification of benefits. In a non-interoperable marketplace, this function typically involves multiple phone calls, facsimile transactions, and manual entry into a registration system. In an e-health environment, this function morphs into an electronic communication. Today, some payers provide online patient verification, thus eliminating follow-up phone calls and facsimile activity.

During each of the hospital's five patient registration avenues, it needed to communicate with the *precertification* and *utilization review* components of the appropriate payers system. If the payer denied the service prior to providing the care, the patient and/or the provider could initiate an appeal.

EXHIBIT 5.13   DATA BEHAVIORAL ANALYSIS: ROUTE OF
PATIENT ADMISSION

Data Library	Checklist	Activity	Key Topic
Collect relevant information	audit	determine scope	high denial rate
	existence	document information	incorrect registration
	identification	label each activity	each mode of admission
	definition	define the activity	flowcharts
	use	define the uses	operational functions
Set benchmarks	source	define route of source	data movement
	value	define (non) & monetary	payment denials $ 15%
	partition	define segmentation	flowcharts
	map	define route of all	flowcharts
	testing	confirm understanding	interviews system review
	redefine	make adjustments	modify flowcharts
	mine	determine intelligence	review outstanding receivables
	modeling	confirm understanding	trend-denial patterns
	output	measure values	measure by source of admission
	response	test values	flowchart error response
	action	measure outcomes	develop internal controls
	implementation	define procedures	measure by source of admission
	next response	reevaluate infrastructure	test system changes
	consequence	measure adverse outcomes	trend-denial patterns
	solutions	redefine scope	adjust process

New Data	Checklist	Activity	Key Topic
Management reports	neural network	subject matter segmentation	measure by source of admission
	hidden patterns	data processing	changes in denials
	deductive	output intelligence	process issues
	predictive	output intelligence	system issues
	information	new audit scope	data-driven decisions

More New Data	Checklist	Activity	Key Topic
	output	measure values	monitoring activity
	analysis	information	

Processed Data	Checklist	Activity	Key Topic
	clustering	information segments	
	neuronsetiology	information details	
		information intelligence	

Data Warehouse	Checklist	Activity	Key Topic
Cyclical patterns feed data Library	outputs	mearsure values	monitoring activity
	center points	benchmarks	
	components	dataflow	
	elements	data dictionary	
	algorithm	data methodology	

EXHIBIT 5.14   **ACCOUNTS RECEIVABLE PIPELINE**

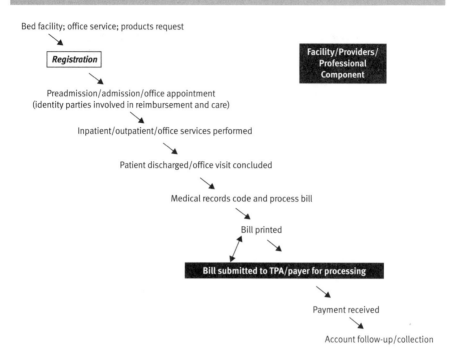

ALGORITHM SELECTION

Several types of algorithms are commonly taught in computer science programs. The following analysis provides an overview of key types of algorithms. The first type is a *simple recursive algorithm*. *Recursive* refers to a characteristic in the formula or configuration that defines a series of steps that can be applied repeatedly. At times, the simple recursive algorithm will have a loop-like effect. An algorithm of this type can be linear in nature, having a loop effect within one set of procedures. Recursive algorithms can also have a branch-like effect, in which algorithm rules involve a series of loops.

Within a hospital patient registration process, one would apply a recursive algorithm if only one mode of registration existed. When more than one mode of registration exists, as in my case study, the recursive algorithms would involve a branch-like format due to the complexity and

EXHIBIT 5.15   **PAYER ACCOUNTS RECEIVABLE PIPELINE**

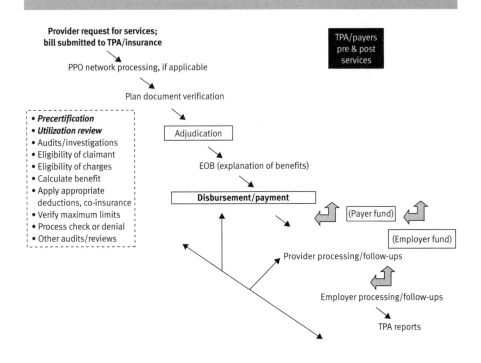

variety of the patient admission process. However, programming solely based on recursive algorithms becomes inefficient when the design involves multiple recursive loops that may limit the ability to gather conclusive information. Therefore, this type of algorithm is more useful as a conceptual tool than as a computational tool.[6]

A second type of algorithm is called *backtracking*. The backtracking methodology walks through a series of decisions until the correct one is found.[7]

Common use of this type of algorithm occurs when a series of decisions exists without necessarily having enough information to make an informed selection. As decisions and selections occur, the algorithm generates new information that impacts subsequent decisions. The algorithm eventually might provide one or more solutions.

Exhibit 5.7 illustrates the use of a backtracking algorithm during the course of patient admission for outpatient services. When patients attempt to register for services at a hospital, the first decision determines what type of service they require. Although patients may have a clear under-standing of what type of service a doctor has ordered for them, if they forget to bring their prescription with them, a hospital cannot proceed because it lacks written confirmation. The registration process there-fore redirects to search for written confirmation. The outcome may be denial of services if documentation cannot be obtained. Upon complet-ing documentation of services ordered from the treating physician, the registrar then gathers health insurance information. Exhibit 5.7 also illus-trates decision-making scenarios for obtaining insurance information. The incremental movement within the 16 workflows presented leads closer to obtaining a solution to the problem presented or the workflow task.

A third algorithm is called *divide and conquer*. A divide-and-conquer algorithm includes the following dynamics:

- Deriving output directly from incremental components
- Dividing large instances into smaller ones, and (recursively) apply-ing the algorithm to the smaller instances
- Combining solutions for the subinstances, to produce a solution for the original instance[8]

This type of algorithm is programmed with two or more recursive commands of the data elements. As its name suggests, this algorithm *divides* "a given problem into two subproblems (ideally of approximately equal size)" and *conquers* "each subproblem (directly or recursively)." It then aggregates the solutions from the two subproblems into one global solution. The art of this algorithm lies in this last step of the process.[9] In a very simplified application of patient registration, a presenting ques-tion could be: "Why does a hospital have denials from registering patients incorrectly?" This question is initially broken down into the various ave-nues in which patient registration occurs. The strengths and weakness from each route are then compared to generate global solutions to the problem. In my case study, the solution involved improving both person-nel and computerized processes.

A fourth algorithm is called *dynamic programming*. This algorithm type focuses on understanding past results and using them to find new results. They have three general characteristics. The first is that overlapping of sub-problems exists. The second is that optimal substructures are used. The third is that the characters of the algorithm use memorization. The memorization or "memo" function "remembers which arguments it has been called with and the result returned and, if called with the same arguments again, returns the result from its memory rather than recalculating it."[10]

The dynamic programming algorithm can be illustrated with patients who have had prior admissions to a hospital. Regardless of avenue of admission, once hospital staff enters unique patient identification, all prior personal information is retrieved and the need to reenter all such information would dissipate. Each hospital then can retrieve all episodes of care for that patient upon admission and eliminate the problem of patients with multiple identification numbers.

Within the payer system, a dynamic programming algorithm could recognize when a claim is submitted more than once to ensure that insurance companies do not make multiple payments for the same episode of care. During an initial run of this type of algorithm, the process may recognize that on a particular date, an amount was paid for a specific service. Programming then stops any further processing of this claim and would deny a duplicate claim.

A fifth type of algorithm, the *greedy* algorithm, involves optimization. This type of algorithm finds the best solution based on available data and has several phases. The first phase involves taking the best information available at a certain point in time without consideration of a future consequence. The algorithm results in the optimal solution based on the available data.

A good example to illustrate a greedy algorithm is the patient registration process for the ER. Hospitals rely on a process called *triage* to select patients for treatment based on the level of acuity rather than order of arrival. A patient with a minor flu may have to wait behind a patient who subsequently arrives with multiple internal injuries from an auto accident. Triage, however, does not always produce optimal results. For instance, a patient who initially was thought to have merely the flu may in fact have a life-threatening clot that is causing a lethargic, general malaise condition.

Another optimization algorithm is called *branch and bound*. This type of algorithm is useful when a root problem exists and an incremental approach to the data produces subproblems to further delineate issues. As the data is processed, results tie back to the presenting problem (a node). If a result does not relate to the node, the algorithm identifies a new issue and creates a new node.

For example, when auditing a group of pharmacy claims, an original root problem could involve isolating prescriptions dispensed more than once in a given day. Data output could demonstrate patterns where the same pharmacy dispenses more than one prescription per day (node A) or multiple pharmacies are dispensing the same medication to the same patient more than once per day (node B). Additional analysis or branches evaluate whether the complicating issue lies directly with the pharmacy claim processing system (node A) or whether resolving the issue requires a better understanding of the patient involved (node B) (i.e., how is a patient able to obtain the same prescription at more than one pharmacy?).

The antithesis of the branch-and-bound approach is the *brute force* algorithm. This type of algorithm is also optimizing in nature and combines all data elements into the analytical process until it obtains a satisfactory result.

For example, imagine an audit that requires the identification of the top 10 medications dispensed in the pharmaceutical claim file on a Friday night. Although the prescribed medications may in fact have an appropriate diagnosis, further audits of highly abused drugs may lead to further discovery. In evaluating these highly abused drugs, an audit question of why they are frequently dispensed on a Friday night versus any other night of the week may be worthy of consideration.

Finally, an auditor can use a *randomized* algorithm to process data elements that lack a definite aim or particular pattern. Using the pharmaceutical claim audit cited above as an example, one algorithm could run a query on the top 10 medications dispensed on a Friday. Another data question might involve the average amount spent per month per employee on medication. For example, Xanax and Vicodin are commonly abused medications to treat anxiety and pain. Would it be coincidental that people need to fill a prescription on a Friday night? Would it be coincidental that one pharmacy in particular has a disproportionate share of patients seeking relief on a Friday night? The aggregation of this data can generate the information necessary to conduct more focused audits for specific findings.

AUDITOR IMPLICATION OVERVIEW

An algorithm is a defined set of steps devoted to a specific purpose and can be categorized by scope or process. Which specific algorithm auditors use to solve a problem will depend on the information available to them and will often change in scope or procedure when new data is generated. Algorithms can drive e-health infrastructures to answer the *who, what, where, why,* and *how* of a healthcare episode at any given time.

As a recap (and an auditor's checklist), thus far we have explored the market background of e-health initiatives, e-health industry applications between and among public and private users, market standards and compliance requirements, clinical and financial case management, data element activity, and algorithms. The next chapter builds on these concepts by delving into data-driven health decision-making processes and their impact on e-health.

ENDNOTES

1. Douglas Harper, "Algorithm," *Online Etymology Dictionary,* Jan. 19, 2008, <Dictionary.com http://dictionary.reference.com/browse/algorithm>.
2. Gerald Toomer, "Al-Khwārizmī, Abu Jafar Muhammad ibn Mūsā," *Dictionary of Scientific Biography 7,* ed. Charles Coulston Gillispie (New York: Charles Scribner's Sons), 358–365.
3. Peter L. Bernstein, *Against the Gods: The Remarkable Story of Risk* (New York: John Wiley & Sons, 1996).
4. Ibid., p. 26.
5. http://www.lubrizol.com/products/passenger-car-oil/default.asp.
6. Ivan Stojmenonvic, "Recursive Algorithms in Computer Science Courses: Fibonacci Numbers and Binomial Coefficients," 1999, Department of Computer Science, University of Ottawa, Ottawa, ON KIN 6N5 Canada.
7. http://www.cis.upenn.edu/~matuszek/cit594-2006/Lectures/27-backtracking.ppt#276,2,A short list of categories.
8. http://www.cse.ohio-state.edu/~gurari/course/cis680/cis680Ch18.html.
9. http://www.cs.ust.hk/faculty/golin/COMP271Sp03/Notes/L03.pdf.
10. Denis Howe, "Memo Function," *The Free On-line Dictionary of Computing,* Jan. 21, 2008, <Dictionary.com http://dictionary.reference.com/browse/memo function>.

CHAPTER 6

Data-Driven Health Decisions in an E-Health Environment

To improve is to change; to be perfect is to change often.

—WINSTON CHURCHILL (1874–1965), BRITISH POLITICIAN

ata-driven decision-making models are emerging in almost every industry sector. This chapter will provide examples of the types of models used in healthcare as well as those models used by other industries that the healthcare industry can learn from. Data, as explained in Chapter 4, is defined and undefined information and appears in various formats, such as *captured results, statistics,* and *records.*

E-health transmits information, once confined to paper, into a virtual world. In the context of e-health, the term *driven* refers to the purposeful capture of data elements to provide the necessary understanding to achieve a particular goal, objective, or purpose. E-health therefore drives electronically programmed and stored data elements related to active functions and operations within the healthcare continuum to derive a conclusion, a judgment, or a determination.

E-health creates the cyber-infrastructure required for a truly interoperable environment for current and emerging market players within the HCC. A fragmented data infrastructure transferred into a fragmented digital world will provide little tangible value and merely overwhelm our current system. The key to an effective, data-driven decision-making

EXHIBIT 6.1 **ORGANIZATIONAL AUDIT CHECKLIST**

Checklist	Chapter
Define the current status of e-health within your environment.	1
Define the current status of e-health among your external relationships.	1
Define members within the healthcare continuum (HCC) that impact your organization.	1
Define the market policies with which your organization must be in compliance.	1
Define the current information continuum (IC) infrastructure.	1
Profile public users of your information.	2
Profile private users of your information.	2
Profile e-source data use, data tools, internal controls.	2
Profile current capacity of your IC.	2
Identify IC issues such as development tools, standard open interfaces, interoperability, code reduction, scalability, reliability, and security.	2
Incorporate market professional standards and regulatory requirements.	2
Acquire applicable market certifications.	2
Identify patient clinical decision-making process.	3
Identify patient financial decision-making process.	3
Define appropriate data fields.	4
Define an applicable data library.	4
Define the process to manage new data.	4
Define the process to manage more new data.	4
Define the process to manage processed data.	4
Define the attributes of the data warehouse.	4
Identify current algorithms within the e-health continuum.	5
Identify and separate effective and ineffective algorithms.	5
Identify required algorithms for development.	5
Categorize each algorithm by type.	5

model is information organization. Exhibit 6.1 pulls together key subjects discussed thus far to provide auditors with an *organizational audit checklist*.

KNOWLEDGE MODELS

Effective electronic data-driven decisions require well-developed knowledge models. The algorithm processes described in Chapter 5 provide tools to organize data elements to collaboratively provide productive information. Several types of *ladders* within defined networks are utilized to develop a framework for a specific knowledge model.

Primary Healthcare Continuum

The primary healthcare continuum (P-HCC) in Exhibit 6.2 illustrates the network of key market players involved in the movement of health and financial information during an episode of care.

To understand the significance of knowledge models within the data-driven decision process, let us look at each ladder through the lens of the patient, as illustrated in Exhibit 6.3.

EXHIBIT 6.2   **PRIMARY HEALTHCARE CONTINUUM**

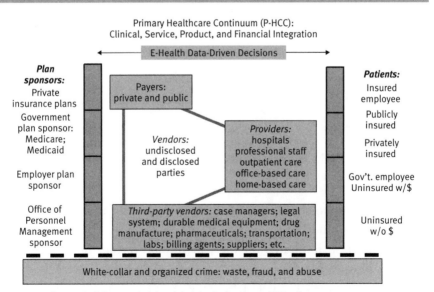

Primary Healthcare Continuum (P-HCC):
Clinical, Service, Product, and Financial Integration

E-Health Data-Driven Decisions

Plan sponsors:
Private insurance plans
Government plan sponsor: Medicare; Medicaid
Employer plan sponsor
Office of Personnel Management sponsor

Payers: private and public

Vendors: undisclosed and disclosed parties

Providers: hospitals professional staff outpatient care office-based care home-based care

Third-party vendors: case managers; legal system; durable medical equipment; drug manufacture; pharmaceuticals; transportation; labs; billing agents; suppliers; etc.

Patients:
Insured employee
Publicly insured
Privately insured
Gov't. employee
Uninsured w/$
Uninsured w/o $

White-collar and organized crime: waste, fraud, and abuse

Segmented, Fragmented, Insulated, Lacks Service and Price Transparency

Source: MBA Inc. (www.mbanews.com; copyright 2007).

EXHIBIT 6.3   **PATIENT CONCEPT LADDER**

| **What types of patients exist within the healthcare continuum?** |

- Active insured employee
- Retired insured employee
- Publicly insured (government sponsored)
- Privately insured (independent)
- Government employee
- Uninsured with assets ($)
- Uninsured without assets ($)
- Uninsured minor

EXHIBIT 6.4   **PATIENT COMPOSITION LADDER**

| What is the composition of patients within the healthcare continuum? |

Insured Employee Active:	**Insured Employee Retired:**	**Publicly Insured:**	**Privately Insured:**
• Type of insurance— ERISA or state insurance plan	• Type of insurance— ERISA or state insurance plan	• Medicare	• Type of insurance
• Contracted or noncontracted carrier	• Secondary coverage	• Medicaid	• Coverage limitations
• E-resources	• E-resources	• Other	• Contracted or noncontracted carrier
		• E-resources	• E-resources

Government Employee:	**Uninsured with Assets:**	**Uninsured without Assets:**	**Uninsured Minor:**
• Coverage limitations	• Market standards for uninsured	• Charity care	• Charity care
• Contracted or noncontracted carrier	• E-resources	• Secondary public and private resources	• Secondary public and private resources
• E-resources		• E-resources	• E-resources

Auditors must first identify and define all market players within the network to be audited or reviewed. Then auditors must isolate each specific player, as illustrated for the patient, and further break down the segments within that node. A more detailed composition ladder is then required to ensure that a data table exists to process identified variables. Exhibit 6.4 illustrates the patient composition ladder.

EXHIBIT 6.5   PATIENT DECISION-MAKING LADDER

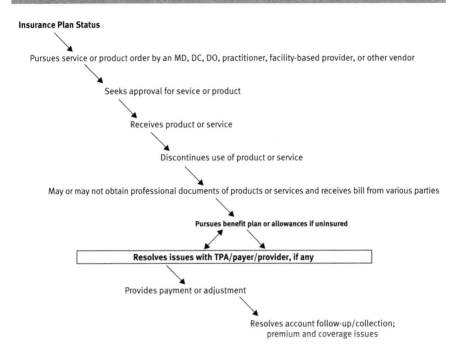

Next, the auditor must consider the patient's decision-making process and test an algorithm to ensure that the electronically defined process proceeds analogously to the actual. Exhibit 6.5 illustrates the typical flow of the patient decision-making ladder.

Insured patients, for instance, are covered for services under the plan and must pay out-of-pocket for services not covered. Plan provisions must therefore be programmed into an information infrastructure. Similarly, an algorithm must identify services not covered by the plan provisions so that during a request for approval or confirmation, the algorithm triggers the message "no coverage." Exhibit 6.6 illustrates coverage determination within an e-environment.

Auditors must focus on how an electronic system handles the coverage determination or a deviation. A coverage determination response (e.g., service not covered) creates data output that derives value beyond

EXHIBIT 6.6   **PATIENT DECISION-MAKING LADDER: ATTRIBUTES AND PROCESS**

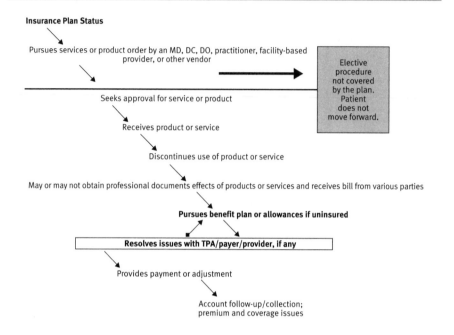

executing the task at hand. For example, with this data in hand, answers to the following questions can be attained:

- How many patients request this service?
- How many plans do not cover this service?
- How many patients seek independent financing of this service?

E-health also provides significant opportunities to exploit the data generation of a process. Auditors should therefore also analyze each process to determine any missing data–gathering opportunities. An overview of a knowledge model includes the components applied in the patient example noted in Exhibit 6.7.

Developing knowledge models for each player within the health continuum is similar to that of the patient model. Developing a provider knowledge model thus begins by identifying the market players, isolating a specific node, and creating a concept ladder listing types of providers

EXHIBIT 6.7   KNOWLEDGE MODEL FRAMEWORK

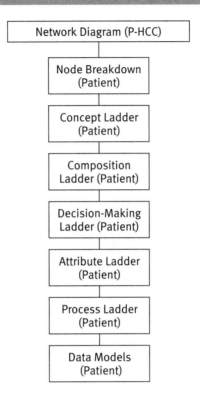

to identify both the facility and the professional components involved. Exhibit 6.8 illustrates a provider concept ladder.

Providers have two subcomponents: (1) the facility in which the service occurs and (2) the professional who performs the service. Each is treated distinctly from a reimbursement perspective. Exhibit 6.9 illustrates the provider composition ladder.

Exhibit 6.10 illustrates the provider decision-making model. The components listed in the exhibit are typical operational steps in a provider environment. How these components are executed from a technological perspective will vary from one provider entity to another. Auditors must therefore define the IC for each market entity reviewed or evaluated.

The provider decision-making flow for an insured patient seeking service for a noncovered item in an e-environment is illustrated in Exhibit 6.11. Generating optimal data intelligence, as noted in the patient model, is the final component of a knowledge model.

EXHIBIT 6.8   **PROVIDER CONCEPT LADDER**

What types of providers exist within the healthcare continuum?

Facilities may be classified as:
- Acute-care inpatient facility
- Outpatient facility
- Same-day surgical center
- Nursing home
- Extended long-term care facility
- Rehabilitation facility
- Home-based care
- Psychiatric facility

Professionals may be classified as:
- Medical doctor (MD)
- Doctor of osteopathy (DO)
- Chiropractic doctor (DC)
- Dentist (DDS)
- Nurse practitioner (NP)
- Physical therapist (PT)

EXHIBIT 6.9   **PROVIDER COMPOSITION LADDER**

What is the composition of providers within the healthcare continuum?

Provider defined as a *facility*:

- Correctly identify the type of facility involved.

- Identify the customer mix or type of patients treated within each facility.

- Identify the e-information infrastructure.

Provider defined as a *professional*:

- Correctly identify the type of credential professionals involved.

- Identify the customer mix or type of patients treated by each professional.

- Identify the e-information infrastructure.

EXHIBIT 6.10   **PROVIDER DECISION-MAKING LADDER**

Bed facility; office service; products request

Registration

Preadmission/admission/office appointment
(identify parties involved in reimbursement and care)

Inpatient/outpatient/office services performed

Patient discharged/office visit concluded

Medical records code and process bill

Bill printed

Bill submitted to TPA/payer for processing

Payment received

Account follow-up/collection

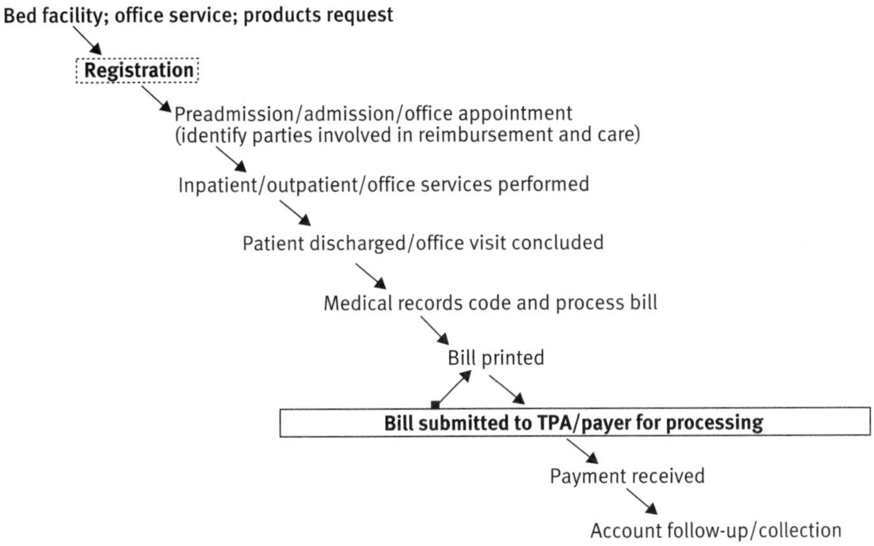

EXHIBIT 6.11   **PROVIDER DECISION-MAKING LADDER:
ATTRIBUTES AND PROCESS**

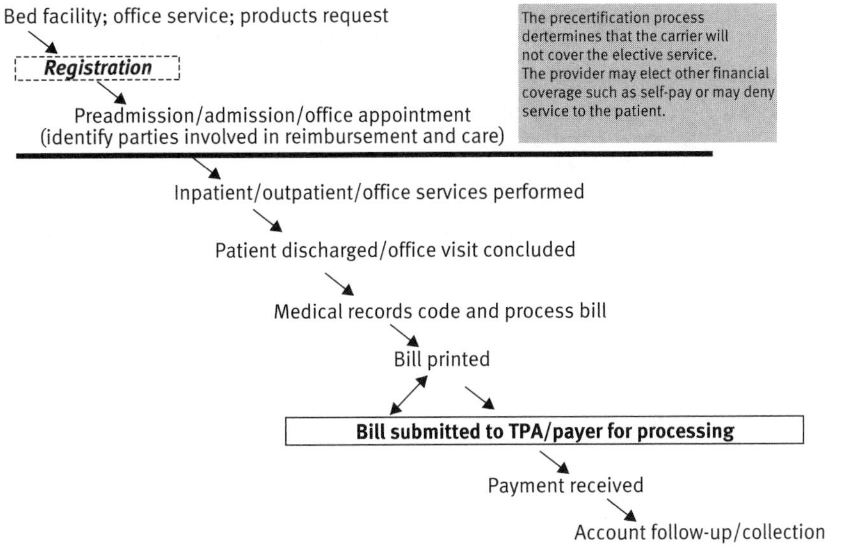

Bed facility; office service; products request

Registration

The precertification process dertermines that the carrier will not cover the elective service. The provider may elect other financial coverage such as self-pay or may deny service to the patient.

Preadmission/admission/office appointment
(identify parties involved in reimbursement and care)

Inpatient/outpatient/office services performed

Patient discharged/office visit concluded

Medical records code and process bill

Bill printed

Bill submitted to TPA/payer for processing

Payment received

Account follow-up/collection

EXHIBIT 6.12   KNOWLEDGE MODEL FRAMEWORK

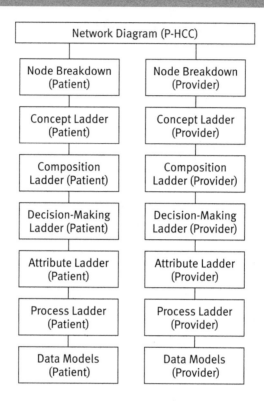

As auditors identify additional market players within an e-environment, the general knowledge model will expand. Adding the provider model to the patient model expands the knowledge model framework, as illustrated in Exhibit 6.12.

The next series of exhibits illustrate application of the knowledge model profiles to payers. Exhibit 6.13 provides the characteristics for consideration for the payer concept ladder.

When an insured patient requests a noncovered service, the process may, for example, identify the payer involved to be a *third-party administrator* (TPA) with a self-insured employer client. Exhibit 6.14 illustrates a payer composition ladder.

Exhibit 6.15 illustrates the payer decision-making process for the case where the payer involved in a transaction is a TPA hired by a self-insured employer that provides healthcare benefits to its employees.

EXHIBIT 6.13   PAYER CONCEPT LADDER

> **What types of payers exist in the healthcare continuum?**

A payer operating as a third-party administrator (TPA):

- With insurance business

- Without insurance business

- With public plan–sponsored programs as clients

- Without public plan–sponsored programs as clients

A payer operating as an insurance company:

- With private employers as clients

- Without private employers as clients

- With government-sponsored programs as clients

- Without government-sponsored programs as clients

EXHIBIT 6.14   PAYER COMPOSITION LADDER

> **What is the composition of payers within the healthcare continuum?**

Payer defined as an *entity* that processes claims submitted by the provider:

- Identify the type of claims-paying agent, which may include:
  - An entity that is hired only by government-sponsored programs
  - An entity that is hired by government-sponsored programs and self-insured employers
  - An entity that is hired by government-sponsored programs, self-insured employers, and sells insurance programs to private-sponsored programs
  - An entity that is hired only by self-insured employers providing health benefits on behalf of their employees

- Identify the provider network and respective contracted fee schedules.

- Identify which programs are subject to ERISA federal government mandates and/or state insurance requirements.

- Identify the e-information infrastructure.

EXHIBIT 6.15   **PAYER DECISION-MAKING LADDER**

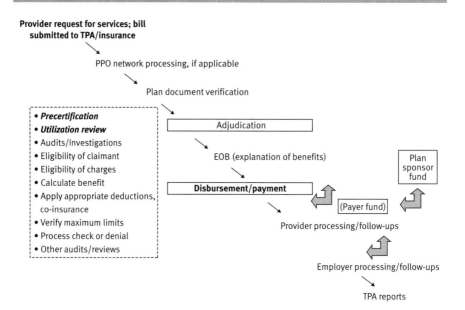

Assuming that an active relationship exists between a TPA and a plan sponsor, the payer decision-making ladder starts with a request for service. The TPA usually receives the request for service directly from a patient or a provider. If the request for service is for an elective procedure, then denial can actually occur at three points: (1) during the request itself; (2) during plan document verification; or (3) if the claim is accepted and/or processed during plan document verification, as illustrated in Exhibit 6.16, then denial can result from adjudication procedures.

Exhibit 6.17 illustrates a plan sponsor concept ladder. For example, when a request for noncovered services occurs, an employee will be classified under a private ERISA plan without supplemental coverage. The plan sponsor composition ladder illustrated in Exhibit 6.18 does not vary much from the payer composition ladder.

The key issue lies in correctly identifying the composition of the plan sponsor. For instance, during a self-insured employer audit, a review of contract terms brought to light the fact that the employer's particular plan actually intertwined ERISA concepts with insurance provisions. The employer operated under the assumption of self-insured status

EXHIBIT 6.16   **PAYER DECISION-MAKING LADDER:
ATTRIBUTES AND PROCESS**

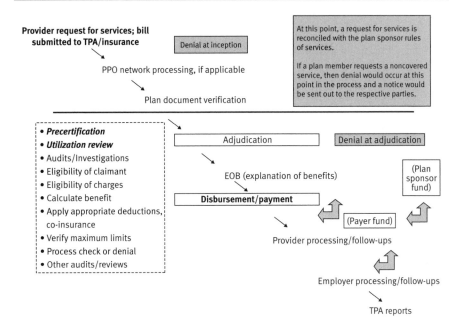

(ERISA plan) when the TPA insurance carrier actually operated as if it offered an insurance program to the employer. Identifying payer composition is important, because compliance requirements and plan rules may vary between state insurance laws and those mandated under ERISA. Exhibit 6.19 illustrates the typical decision-making ladder for plan sponsors.

Plan sponsors should define services to be covered prior to implementing their benefit program (services mandated by legislation, such as obstetrical care, cannot be excluded from any plan). If the TPA uses auto-adjudication processes, the auditor must verify all electronically programmed inclusions or exclusions. Because requests for services are electronically processed without human intervention, testing of the accuracy of those tables is very important. Exhibit 6.20 illustrates the result for a patient who requests an elective service not covered by the plan sponsor.

Exhibit 6.21 illustrates the addition of the payer (TPA) and plan sponsor to the patient and provider knowledge model for handling requested services.

EXHIBIT 6.17   **PLAN SPONSOR CONCEPT LADDER**

What types of plan sponsors exist in the healthcare continuum?

Plan sponsors include:
- Private insurance plan (state governed?)
- Self-insured plan (ERISA governed?)
- Government plan sponsors
  - Medicare
  - Medicaid
  - **Champus**
  - Child health insurance
  - Veteran programs
- Government employee program
- Employer-sponsored program
  - ERISA plan
  - Insurance plan

If patient has more than one plan sponsor, identify both:
- Medicare with private supplemental insurance
- Private plan with supplemental insurance
- Multiple plans for different coverage
  - Catastrophic versus long-term care
  - Drug cards

EXHIBIT 6.18   **PLAN SPONSOR COMPOSITION LADDER**

What is the composition for the plan sponsors noted within the healthcare continuum?

Plan sponsor defined as an entity that is funding healthcare benefits for a defined beneficiary group of individuals:
- Identify the type of plan sponsor, which may include:
  - An entity defined as a publicly held employer
  - An entity defined as a privately held employer with 20 or more employees
  - An entity defined as a privately held employer with 20 or less employees
  - An entity defined as a collective group of individually insured participants
  - An entity sponsored by a government program such as Medicare, Medicaid, CHIPS, Veterans, etc.
  - An entity defined as a public agency providing government employees' health benefits

- Identify the provider network and respective contracted fee schedules.
- Identify which programs are subject to ERISA, federal government mandates, and/or state insurance requirements.
- Identify the e-information infrastructure.

EXHIBIT 6.19   **PLAN SPONSOR DECISION-MAKING LADDER**

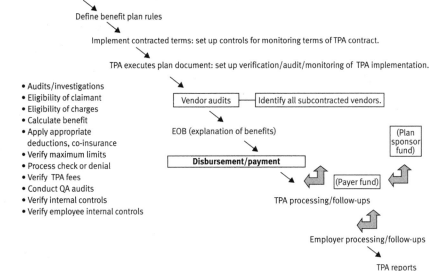

EXHIBIT 6.20   **PLAN SPONSOR DECISION-MAKING LADDER: ATTRIBUTES AND PROCESS**

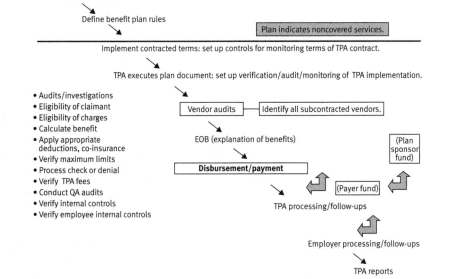

EXHIBIT 6.21   KNOWLEDGE FRAMEWORK: HANDLING
REQUESTED SERVICES

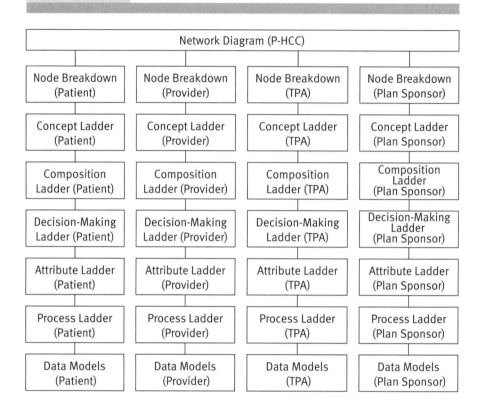

Secondary Healthcare Continuum

Analysis of applicable market and policy issues within the context of the secondary healthcare continuum (S-HCC), illustrated in Exhibit 6.22, impacts the knowledge model's framework.

When a patient requests a noncovered elective service, S-HCC issues for consideration may include public policy, ERISA requirements, and state insurance requirements. Another consideration may be the case management function, such as payer or provider provision of financial case management services. The process of blending of P-HCC and S-HCC

EXHIBIT 6.22   **SECONDARY HEALTHCARE CONTINUUM**

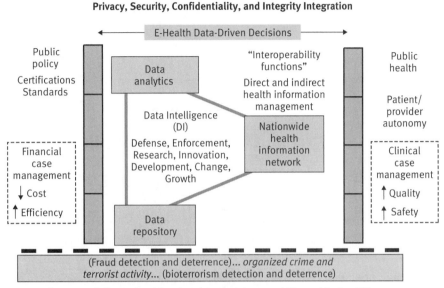

Segmented, Fragmented, Insulated, Lacks Interoperability and Optimal DI

distinct market services will integrate operational issues that may overlap, such as the benefit plan design (P-HCC) that may be modified as a result of any relevant policy issues or mandates (S-HCC).

Information Continuum

The information continuum (IC), illustrated in Exhibit 6.23, is the third layer to be accounted for and included in the knowledge model.

The IC impacts the knowledge network because of the electronic communication tools and infrastructure necessary for handling requests for service.

To recap, auditors develop the knowledge model framework by identifying applicable components (based on the presenting task or operational activity) of three networks: the P-HCC, S-HCC, and the IC. They then break down any *information nodes* selected (e.g., patient, provider, payer, and plan sponsor). Development of a concept and composition ladder for each node follows. The creation of a decision-making model then highlights the operational activities of each node. Identification of attributes

EXHIBIT 6.23 INFORMATION CONTINUUM

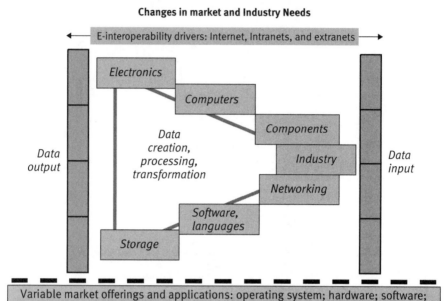

Segmented, Fragmented, Insulated, Non-par Application and Pace

and process indicates at which point the presenting issue impacts the decision-making model. Finally, the disposition of the task provides a database for future analysis of the defined knowledge network. The outline of a knowledge model for handling requested services is illustrated in Exhibit 6.24.

THIRD-PARTY VENDOR KNOWLEDGE MODEL

The term *third-party vendors* refers to the large number of nonprofessional or facility-based care providers that offer health-related products or services such as durable medical equipment (DME), pharmaceuticals, pharmaceutical benefit managers (PBMs), ambulances, case managers, and attorneys. Exhibit 6.25 illustrates the third-party vendor concept ladder.

The breakdown of this node depends on the specific type of vendor. Exhibit 6.26 illustrates the third-party vendor composition ladder.

EXHIBIT 6.24   KNOWLEDGE MODEL FRAMEWORK: HANDLING REQUESTED SERVICES

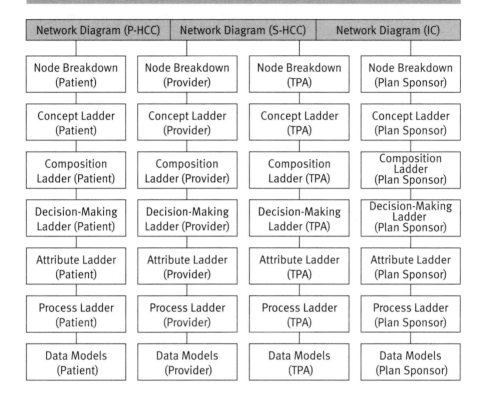

The third-party vendor decision-making model illustrated in Exhibit 6.27 recognizes that patients who request a noncovered service might finance the service without plan sponsor approval.

Consider the decision-making ladder for the movement of pharmaceuticals as illustrated Exhibit 6.28. Auditors would identify the pharmaceutical distribution network and existing nodes within the primary healthcare continuum. A concept ladder and composition ladder would further detail subcomponents within the network. Auditors would then use the secondary healthcare continuum to identify the applicable policies

EXHIBIT 6.25   **THIRD-PARTY VENDOR CONCEPT LADDER**

What types of third-party vendors exist within the healthcare continuum?

Vendors may include:

- Professionals
  - Case managers
  - Allied health professionals
  - Legal professionals
- Durable medical equipment
- Pharmaceuticals
- Transportation
- Billing agents
- Suppliers
- Manufacturers

What are the specific market considerations for each type of vendor?

EXHIBIT 6.26   **THIRD-PARTY VENDOR COMPOSITION LADDER**

What is the composition of third-party vendors within the healthcare continuum?

Third-party vendor defined as an *entity* that is supporting any other market player within the P-HCC:

- Correctly identify the type of vendor, which may include:
  - Product services
    - Manufacturer of products
    - Manufacturer of pharmaceuticals
    - Retail support
    - PBM—pharmacy benefit management program
  - Professional support
    - Case managers
    - Attorneys
    - Outsourced staff support, such as renal dialysis
  - Technical support
    - Billing agents
    - Transportation
    - Audit and IT support
- Identify the provider network and respective contracted fee schedules.
- Identify which programs are subject to ERISA, federal government mandates, and/or state insurance requirements.
- Identify the e-information infrastructure.

EXHIBIT 6.27   THIRD-PARTY VENDOR DECISION-MAKING LADDER: ATTRIBUTES AND PROCESS

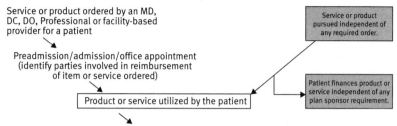

Service or product ordered by an MD, DC, DO, Professional or facility-based provider for a patient

Service or product pursued independent of any required order.

Preadmission/admission/office appointment (identify parties involved in reimbursement of item or service ordered)

Product or service utilized by the patient

Patient finances product or service independent of any plan sponsor requirement.

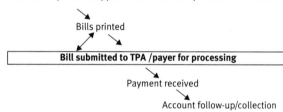

Patient discontinues use of product or service.

Ordering professional documents effects of products or services and processes bill or professional component. Supplier submit a bill for product or services.

Bills printed

Bill submitted to TPA /payer for processing

Payment received

Account follow-up/collection

EXHIBIT 6.28   PHARMACEUTICAL DECISION-MAKING LADDER

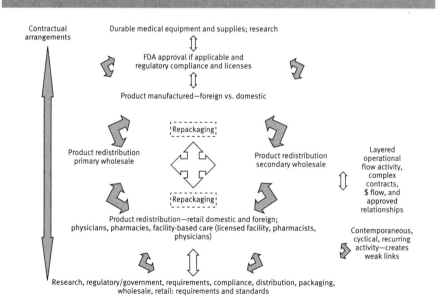

Contractual arrangements

Durable medical equipment and supplies; research

FDA approval if applicable and regulatory compliance and licenses

Product manufactured—foreign vs. domestic

Repackaging

Product redistribution primary wholesale

Product redistribution secondary wholesale

Layered operational flow activity, complex contracts, $ flow, and approved relationships

Repackaging

Product redistribution—retail domestic and foreign; physicians, pharmacies, facility-based care (licensed facility, pharmacists, physicians)

Contemporaneous, cyclical, recurring activity—creates weak links

Research, regulatory/government, requirements, compliance, distribution, packaging, wholesale, retail: requirements and standards impacting the pharmaceutical industry. Finally, auditors would use the information continuum to identify the technological infrastructure in which pharmaceuticals operate.

KNOWLEDGE MODELS FOR WHITE-COLLAR AND ORGANIZED CRIME

White-collar and organized crime share common attributes of deceit and lawlessness. However, each type is distinct with respect to its attributes and components. Attributes and components can be broken down into the following categories: activity, organization, and system. Activity may involve crimes committed by the affluent or individuals in a position of influence in the normal course of business. They tend to be self-dealing in nature. The attributes of these activities may include medical identity theft, identity theft, sale of medically unnecessary *legitimate* medications, health products, and procedures; sale of *counterfeit* medications, health products, and procedures; illegal and unethical marketing and recruitment schemes; stealing resources and money from government programs, provider delivery systems, payer systems, and vendor systems; intrastate in international theft of all of the above activity. Additional activities may include embezzlement; misappropriation of resources; collusion, price-fixing, false advertising; illegal pollution; false financials; substandard products; illegal tax avoidance; illegal sale of unsafe products; illegal unsafe working conditions; misrepresentation of professionals, product, service; false research; sale of unnecessary medical services; kickbacks; undisclosed commissions; other financial misrepresentations and-or falsifications.

The organizational component can simply be one individual or collective group of individuals on behalf of the organization. The system component of the crime can be stand alone or intermingle with legitimate business activity. Attributes of the system may include banking systems, executive office, licensed professionals, industry-specific vendors, employers, healthcare and payer systems, electronic mediums, laws and regulations by country.

Because the healthcare marketplace generates trillions of dollars, crime must be, at minimum, recognized as a potential issue in any e-audit plan. The criminal statistics and monetary impact speak for themselves. A report published by the FBI entitled *Financial Crimes Report to the Public Fiscal Year 2006*[1] noted the following staggering statistics:

- In 2005, 8.3 million cases of identity theft were reported (3.7% of adult population)
- Over 200 million hours were spent in attempting to recover from identity theft.
- Increased activity in medical identity theft for false billings or theft of benefits.
- Fraudulent healthcare billing is estimated to involve between 3 and 10 percent of all claims.
- Significant increase in medical data theft.
- Healthcare is expected to exceed $3.3 trillion by 2012.

SAMPLE IDENTITY THEFT CASE

The following high-profile FBI case shows how vulnerable healthcare entities are to theft of medical data and the resulting impact:

HAROLD MCCOY, ET AL. (PHILADELPHIA): On June 16, 2006, Harold McCoy was sentenced to 162 months in prison following a guilty plea to charges of bank fraud, identity theft, and conspiracy for his role in a scheme to defraud numerous American Red Cross (ARC) blood donors in the Philadelphia area. McCoy obtained the names and personal identifying information of numerous blood donors from an employee of ARC. He and his co-conspirators, Karynn Long and Danielle Baker, then used the stolen information to obtain instant credit loans, bank loans, and to cash counterfeit checks, causing approximately $800,000 in losses to various financial institutions. This crime jeopardized the Philadelphia area blood supply and damaged ARC's trusted relationship with the public, as many people stopped donating blood and two corporate donation centers ceased their blood drives when the media reported the crime. For their roles in this scheme, Long pled guilty to bank fraud and conspiracy and was sentenced to 18 months in prison; Baker pled guilty to identity theft and conspiracy and was sentenced to 24 months in prison. All three defendants were ordered to pay restitution in the amount of $270,555.[2]

MEDICAL IDENTITY THEFT

Medical identity theft (MIT) is a type of identity theft relating to the practice of medicine and matters pertaining to general illness or wellness.[3] *Theft* is the act of stealing where an offender obtains unauthorized use or possession of another's property, often via deceptive means or control. In the case of MIT, *property* is defined as the medical identity of an individual that provides access to healthcare monetary or service benefits. MIT can occur at any point in the healthcare continuum.

MIT has evolved since the inception of healthcare benefit programs and is a matter of urgent attention due to the highly adverse effect on individual victims. Healthcare is a high-volume cash industry that goes beyond the commonly discussed patient–provider relationship. To illustrate the magnitude of opportunity for MIT, consider that three months of claims data for one Medicare region can create about one terabyte of activity (equivalent to about 40,000 trees shredded into paper). The P-HCC and S-HCC market participants who use some form of personal health information in their normal course of business create a source for potential MIT vulnerability with every one of their transactions.

In an electronic health environment, auditors need to be on guard for breaches of individual *identifiable health information* (IIHI), documented data elements that comprise an individual's identity. Any electronic health record system should secure the following IIHI elements:[4]

IIHI Elements

1. Names
2. All geographical subdivisions smaller than a state, including street address, city, county, precinct, ZIP Code, and their equivalent geographical codes, except for the initial three digits of a ZIP Code if, according to the current publicly available data from the Bureau of the Census:
   a. The geographical unit formed by combining all ZIP Codes with the same three initial digits contains more than 20,000 people.
   b. The initial three digits of a ZIP Code for all such geographical units containing 20,000 or fewer people are changed to 000.
3. All elements of dates (except year) for dates directly related to an individual, including birthdate, admission date, discharge date, date of death; and all ages over 89 and all elements of dates (including year) indicative of such age, except that such ages and elements may be aggregated into a single category of age 90 or older.
4. Telephone numbers.
5. Facsimile numbers.

6. E-mail addresses.
7. Social security numbers.
8. Medical record numbers.
9. Health plan beneficiary numbers.
10. Account numbers.
11. Certificate/license numbers.
12. Vehicle identifiers and serial numbers, including license plate numbers.
13. Device identifiers and serial numbers.
14. Web universal resource locators (URLs).
15. Internet protocol (IP) address numbers.
16. Biometric identifiers, including fingerprints and voiceprints.
17. Full-face photographic images and any comparable images.
18. Any other unique identifying number, characteristic, or code, unless otherwise permitted by the Privacy laws.

MEDICAL IDENTITY THEFT—DEFINITION

Medical identity theft is the theft of IIHI for the purpose of misrepresentation of health information to obtain access to property or permanently deprive or harm an individual while interacting within the healthcare continuum. Use of an individual's identity outside the healthcare continuum is considered *identity theft*. When a perpetrator steals all or part of the IIHI elements from a medical record file to open up a credit card account and go on a shopping spree, it is considered identity theft—not medical identity theft. The differentiating factor for medical identity theft is that the stolen information is used for illegal gains within the healthcare domain. (See Exhibit 6.29.)

HOW MEDICAL IDENTITY THEFT OCCURS

The movement of protected health information (PHI) within the P-HCC can result in services rendered or products provided and related financial transactions. Key legitimate market players involved in these transactions include the patient, the provider, the payer, the plan sponsor, support vendors that may or may not be disclosed, and third-party vendors. Illicit market players involved include organized and white-collar crime entities. The key defining factor of the P-HCC is the direct provision

EXHIBIT 6.29   MEDICAL IDENTITY THEFT CONTINUUM

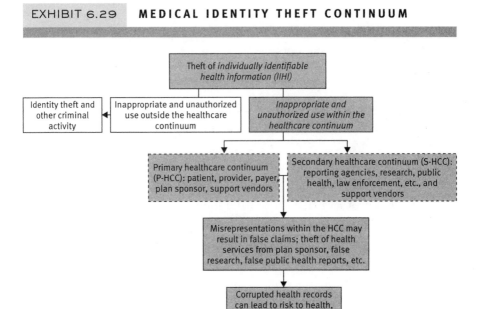

of a service to the patient, but MIT can occur at any point within the P-HCC or S-HCC. Finally, it is important to not exclude nontraditional healthcare providers, such as those for donating blood. The case illustrated earlier of Harold McCoy notes the importance of all health data stored in all healthcare transactions, including the donation of blood.

Another example includes the case of Katrina Brookes. Ms. Brookes started receiving healthcare bills in the name of her son, which included his middle name. At this point no one knew her child's middle name except close family and the hospital in which she completed paperwork to obtain her son's social security number.[5] The new paperwork was not placed within her son's medical record. New bills started to arrive from other providers. The mother was suspicious; how could any other new provider know of her son's middle name since she had not shared it with anyone else? Again, the breach occurred during a nontraditional health service in the healthcare setting. Anyone can be a victim, the elderly, the sick, or the unsuspecting. When it comes to children, however, many of them will not know that their identity has been breached until the age at which they are able to secure credit. With respect to health services, the child will be dependent on the adult to ensure that future providers are not responding to adulterated records. These examples illustrate exposure to financial issues and medical errors issues, but how about losing your children?

The story of Anndorie Sachs, from Salt Lake City and mother of four children, provides an unimaginable consequence of MIT. Her experience dates back to April 2006, when she was approached by a Utah social worker. The plan was to take away her children. The last time Ms. Sachs had given birth to a child was in 2004. The problem was that Dorothy Bell Moran, a known meth user, gave birth with Ms. Sachs's identification at the hospital. Social Services wanted to take away Ms. Sachs's children because they thought she just delivered a baby with meth in her bloodstream. After repeated phone calls for clarification, Ms. Sachs was able to prove that Ms. Moran delivered the baby with meth in her blood+ stream. Ms. Sachs was then allowed to keep her children. Further consequences were noted when Ms. Sachs was later admitted into a different hospital with a kidney infection. The next issue involved Ms. Moran's health records were not integrated into Ms. Sachs record. A critical issue occurred in that Ms. Sachs's blood type is different from Ms. Moran's, thus creating an opportunity for Ms. Sachs to be subjected to a medical error due to incorrect information.[6]

DAMAGES TO PRIMARY VICTIMS

Primary victims or patients face a variety of threats resulting from MIT. Examples of damages to patients include:

- Access denial to future healthcare services resulting from exhausted benefits
- Exposure to medical errors and subsequent demise of health due to integration of perpetrator health data into victim's health data
- Unwarranted litigation due to behaviors and activities by the perpetrator during episodes in which the medical identity was assumed by the perpetrator
- Unwarranted financial damage due to behaviors and activities by the perpetrator during episodes in which the medical identity was assumed by the perpetrator

MEDICAL IDENTITY THEFT FROM A CONSUMER PERSPECTIVE

When the Consumer Is Not Aware

A woman who was affiliated with a medical facility had access to claim forms and medical records. She submitted claims for heart surgery, gall bladder surgery, finger amputations, a hysterectomy, and more—27 surgeries in all. There were no hospitalizations or claims for anesthesia. The woman utilized PHI and assumed the identity (on paper) of several patients to collect money.

When the Consumer Is Involved

At an insurance company, all payments of foreign claims are made to the insured and not to the foreign medical provider. An insured submitted $90,000 in fictitious foreign claims from a clinic in South America, indicating that the entire family was in a car accident. A fictitious police report accompanied the medical claims. A telephone call to the clinic revealed that the insured and the dependents were never treated in their clinic.

When an Individual Wants Products or Services

A man stole Medicaid recipient cards that entitled the bearer to medical benefits, including prescription drugs, paid for by the Medicaid program. He also stole written prescriptions, purportedly issued by doctors for various narcotic medicines, for personal use.[7] He was convicted of Medicaid fraud and receipt of stolen property and faced up to six years in state prison and a fine of up to $20,000.

Deterrence by Consumers[8]

- Shred all explanations of benefits, expired benefit cards, healthcare billing statements, and/or health records prior to discarding them.
- Protect social security numbers, benefit plan ID cards, and any other document that identifies individuals with any healthcare benefit plan.
- Do not give out personal health information on the phone, through mail, or over the Internet unless the party receiving the disclosed information is known and trusted.

- Never click on links sent in unsolicited e-mails.
- Be mindful of free personal health records programs that offer to track information and free health screenings in which they ask for benefit information.
- Do not use obvious passwords like date of birth, name, mother's maiden name, or the last four digits of social security numbers for electronic communications containing health records or benefit claim information.
- Keep all health information and benefit card information in a safe, secure place.
- If you are admitted into a healthcare setting, leave your credit cards and any other identification information at home.
- Do not have your family bring your personal mail to any inpatient facility.
- Be careful when you do visit any clinic to leave your sensitive information in a locked locker.
- Refuse requests for social security numbers. If absolutely required, request how the information will be stored and monitored. Many carriers are not using social security on their identification card.
- Ask your provider to use your medical record number for identification purposes instead of your social security number.
- From time to time, review the content of your medical records for detailed personal information.
- Most important, never be afraid to ask questions. If you do not understand the response, ask for it again.

Detection by Consumers[9]

- Monitor and review explanations of benefits (EOBs).
- Look for bills from providers never seen before.
- Look for bills with ambiguous dates of service.
- Look for bills with ambiguous diagnoses on the EOBs.
- Review explanations of review (EOR) statements in the same manner.
- Review your release of medical records to third parties.
- Check credit reports for any outstanding bills from providers.
- Look for letters from insurance companies regarding denied services for services never requested.

Defense and Mitigation by Consumers[10]

- Place a fraud alert on credit reports. Once perpetrators steal a medical identity, then they may enter into other financial arrangements.
- File a police report and contact providers immediately.
- Obtain copies of medical records and review them for any ambiguous information.
- Work with providers to address any misinformation.
- Report the theft to the Federal Trade Commission.
- Contact your insurance company and request a complete historical claim run. Ask them for a complete listing of any bills submitted in your name with your benefit card.
- Report to your carrier any providers that are on your list that you have never seen before.

DAMAGES TO SECONDARY VICTIMS

Although it is appropriate to view the patient as the central victim in an episode of medical identity theft, secondary victims, including the entities perpetrators breach to gain access to the IIHI, also exist. Examples of damages to secondary victims include:

- Financial loss by any market player who must write off the theft of goods and services to bad debt
- Risk of litigation by the primary victim resulting from theft within your institution
- Financial loss to the plan sponsor for the cost of goods and services

MEDICAL IDENTITY THEFT FROM AN ENTITY'S PERSPECTIVE

When a provider's employee obtains access to IIHI to submit false claims, the provider may be liable to the patient because of the breach of privacy and information. Vulnerability may be enhanced if the entity does not have the appropriate internal controls that could have prevented such an activity from occurring. Providers are also susceptible to financial loss from the use of unwarranted benefits and fraudulent claims when false diagnosis and procedure codes are generated. This type of breach can also be committed at an insurance company by claims personnel.

Deterrence by Entities

- Implement appropriate infrastructure security measures for all electronic and or paper transactions.
- Shred all explanations of benefits, expired benefit cards, healthcare billing statements, and or health records prior to discarding them.
- Use appropriate destruction methods for any electronic storage media prior to discarding them.
- Any systems issues relating to or review of potential security vulnerabilities should meet current market standards and requirements.
- Consider internal control security measures for PHI access and use from each of the P-HCC, S-HCC, and IC perspectives.

Detection by Entities

- Monitor for data conflicts in demographic information of a patient.
- Monitor denials of patient claims based on medical-necessity issues.
- Monitor for unusual use or access of the IIHI elements.
- Monitor patient complaints of missing personal items by department.
- Monitor inventory losses of prescription medications by department.

Defense and Mitigation by Entities

- Create internal policies and implement internal controls for verification of patient identity.
- Test controls on a routine schedule.
- Test systems security to ensure appropriate user access.
- Test and review access logs of users who review patient information that is not directly related to their job function.
- Test and review access logs at the time a patient is registered for any activity by users that is not involved in patient registration.

AUDITOR CONSIDERATIONS

Auditors need to understand how electronic information moves within the healthcare continuum and how data is transferred between market players. *Data integrity of health information* involves internal controls for privacy and security of all IHII elements specifically within the P-HCC and S-HCC, as illustrated in Exhibit 6.29. Policies and practices to prevent, detect, and mitigate MIT should be incorporated through out these healthcare continuums.

Use of stolen IIHI may result in:

- Access to third-party health benefits products or services
- Access to reimbursement funds that result from third-party benefits
- Access to health data to misrepresent health status for disability employment and so on
- Access to health data and assumed medical identity to perpetrate other crimes

SAMPLE FRAUD CASE

Greed without regard for consequence motivates most fraud schemes. The following case illustrates the ultimate consequence—death:

> JORGE A. MARTINEZ, MD (CLEVELAND): This investigation resulted in the first known prosecution involving a criminal charge of Health Care Fraud resulting in death. The case focused on the illegal distribution of pharmaceutical narcotics and billing for unnecessary medical procedures. The investigation revealed that Dr. Martinez provided excessive narcotic prescriptions, including OxyContin, to patients in exchange for the patients enduring unnecessary nerve block injections. Dr. Martinez' actions directly resulted in the death of two of his patients. From 1998 until his arrest in 2004, Martinez submitted more than $59 million in claims to Medicare, Medicaid, and the Ohio Bureau of Worker's Compensation. In January 2006, a jury found Martinez guilty of 56 criminal counts, including distribution of controlled substances, mail fraud, wire fraud, Health Care Fraud, and Health Care Fraud resulting in death. Martinez was later sentenced to life in prison. This investigation was conducted jointly with the HHS-OIG, Ohio Bureau of Workers Compensation, DEA Diversion, AdvanceMed, Ohio Department of Job and Family Services, Anthem Blue Cross Blue Shield and Medical Mutual of Ohio.[11]

SAMPLE PHARMACEUTICAL FRAUD CASE

With the advent of Medicare prescription drug coverage and the high cost of medications, pharmaceutical fraud jumped onto the law enforcement radar screen. The impact, effect, and cost associated with patients receiving medically unnecessary, adulterated, or counterfeit medications are undocumented.

> BANSAL ORGANIZATION (PHILADELPHIA): This investigation was conducted jointly with the DEA and IRS and was focused on a Philadelphia-based Internet pharmacy drug distributor which was smuggling drugs into the U.S. from India and selling them over the Internet. The criminal organization shipped several thousand packages per week to individuals around the country. In April 2005, 24 individuals were indicted on charges of distributing controlled substances, importing controlled substances, involvement in a continuing criminal enterprise, introducing misbranded drugs into interstate commerce, and participating in money laundering. Over $8 million has been seized to date as a result of the charges. As of December 1, 2006, 12 suspects have pled guilty, three have been convicted at trial, four are in foreign custody, and five remain fugitives. This investigation was worked jointly with the DEA, IRS, ICE, USPIS, and the Lower Merion Police Department.[12]

The knowledge model for white-collar and organized crime also begins with a concept ladder. Both types of criminal activities have evolved significantly with respect to the use of technology and highly skilled professionals. Exhibit 6.30 separates the two types of criminal activity.

EXHIBIT 6.30   CONCEPT LADDER

What types of crime exist within the healthcare continuum?

White-collar may include:

- Professional misrepresentation
- Facility misrepresentation
- False billings
- False claims
- Unnecessary medical treatment
- Contractual manipulations

Organized crime may include:

- Medical identity theft
- Prescription drug diversion
- Prescription drug counterfeit
- Accident crime rings
- Pill-mill schemes

EXHIBIT 6.31	WHITE-COLLAR CRIME COMPOSITION LADDER

What is the composition of illicit behavior noted within white-collar crime?

Key Feature	Characterization of White-Collar crime	Modern Technology
Activity	Crimes committed by the affluent or individuals in position of influence in the normal course of business. They tend to be self-dealing in nature.	Embezzlement, misappropriation of resources; collusion, price-fixing, false advertising; illegal pollution; price-fixing; false financials; substandard products; illegal tax avoidance; illegal sale of unsafe products; illegal unsafe working conditions; misrepresentation of professionals, product, service; false research; sale of unnecessary medical services; klickbacks; undisclosed commissions; other financial misrepresentations and/or falsifications.
Organization	Individual or collective on behalf of the organization.	Organization—complex layered, multidisciplined, multiprofessional, and highly skilled.
System	Crime is intermingled with legitimate business activity.	Banking systems, executive office, licensed professionals, industry-specific vendors, employers, healthcare and payer systems, electronic medias, laws and regulations by country.

EXHIBIT 6.32	ORGANIZED CRIME COMPOSITION LADDER

What is the composition of illicit behavior noted within organized crime?

Key Feature	Characterization of Organized Crime	Modern Technology
Activity	Provision of Illegal and stolen goods and services.	Sale of new identities; medical identity theft; sale of medically unnecessary *legitimate* medications, health products, and procedures. Sale of *counterfeit* medications, health products, and procedures. Illegal and unethical marketing and recruitment schemes. Stealing resources and money from government programs, provider delivery systems, payer systems, and vendor systems. Intrastate and international theft in all of the above activities. Various schemes include: rent-a-patient, pill-mill, drop box.
Organization	Complex arrangements.	Organization—complex layered, multidisciplined, multiprofessional, and highly skilled.
System	Integration of legal and illegal structures.	Banking systems, industry-specific vendors, employers, healthcare and payer systems, electronic media, laws and regulations by country.

Exhibit 6.31 addresses the characteristics of white-collar crime activities that tend to be self-dealing in nature. They may occur individually or through collusive behavior among several individuals or entities on behalf of a corporation.

The composition of organized crime activity, illustrated in Exhibit 6.32, focuses on the provision of illegal goods and services or the resale of stolen goods or services.

AUDIT IMPLICATION OVERVIEW

This chapter introduced the elements of data-driven decision-making models as defined within the primary and secondary healthcare continuum that overlap with the information continuum. The e-audit implication is structure, application, and technology. E-health exists today but is evolving rapidly. The concepts presented therefore should be used to identify the structure, application, and technology of the e-system being reviewed through the knowledge model network diagram process.

The algorithms in Chapter 5 provide the opportunity for data mining, data-driven decisions, and the development of artificial intelligence through rule-based systems. The market has numerous niche data-driven e-health decision offerings. Many of them exist in the form of disease management models to fraud detection systems.

The following examples offer perspectives of e-health- and e-data-driven model developments outside of the United States. The most significant discussions and focus are on technological infrastructure and complement the discussions of what is occurring within the United States (see Chapter 2).

EXAMPLES OF WORLDWIDE ACTIVITY

- *Australia:* National E-Health Transition Authority is "a not-for-profit company established by the Australian State and Territory governments to develop better ways of electronically collecting and securely exchanging health information." It defines its purpose as to create "Electronic health information (or e-health) systems that can securely and efficiently exchange data and can significantly improve how important clinical and administrative information is communicated between healthcare professionals . . . to unlock substantially greater quality, safety and efficiency benefits." (http://www.nehta.gov.au)

- *European Union:* European E-Health Research Area is pursuing several objectives "to contribute to the coordination of Member States' eHealth strategy formulation and implementation as well as eHealth-related Research and Technology Development (RTD)." (http://www.ehealth-era.org/index.htm)

- *Africa:* Free Software and Open Source Foundation for Africa (FOSSFA) and organizational activities of the Information Communications Technology for development (ICT4D) are developing e-health strategy frameworks. (www.tossa.org; http://www.fossfa.net)

- *Canada:* E-health initiatives include both administrative and healthcare delivery infrastructures. The Canadians have initiated the development of an electronic health record in addition to activities such as teleconsults, for example, remote monitoring of patients in the home setting. (http://www.hc-sc.gc.ca/hcs-sss/ehealth-esante/index_e.html)

- *Japan:* In 1994, the Japanese Association of Healthcare Information Systems Industry (JAHIS) was established to address e-health initiatives. Its mission includes "promoting the concept of medical information systems, specifically focusing on the development of electronically processing medical images, medical records and receipts." In addition, it focuses on developing standards that will link health, medical, and welfare services. (http://www.itu.int/itudoc/itu-t/workshop/e-health/s9-02.pdf)

- *Mexico:* E-health is integrated into Mexico's e-government system. The National e-Mexico system focuses on integrating the efficiency from technology in which its citizens interact with all facets of government programs. The goal of the e-health initiative is to improve lives; provide access to health information; integrate a digital online dossier; develop a system of epidemiological control; create an electronic information exchange; and communicate on matters of health. (http://www.emexico.gob.mx/wb2/eMex/eMex_eHealth)

- *World Health Organization (WHO)* is the directing and coordinating authority for health within the United Nations system. WHO has developed an eHealth Standardization Coordination Group (eHSCG) to develop "a platform to promote stronger coordination among the key players in all technical areas of e-health standardization. The group is a place for exchange of information and will work towards the creation of cooperation mechanisms to: Identify areas where further standardization is required and try to identify responsibilities for such activities; Provide guidance for implementations and case studies; Consider the requirements for appropriate development paths for health profiles of existing standards from different sources in order to provide functional sets for key health applications; Support activities to increase user awareness of the existing standards, and case studies." (http://www.who.int/ehscg/en/)

ENDNOTES

1. http://www.fbi.gov/publications/financial/fcs_report2006/financial_crime_2006.htm.
2. Ibid.
3. American Psychological Association (APA): "medical" (n.d.), *Dictionary.com Unabridged (v 1.1)*, retrieved March 06, 2008, website: http://dictionary.reference.com/browse/medical.
4. http://privacyruleandresearch.nih.gov/pr_08.asp#8a.
5. http://www.msnbc.msn.com/id/23392229.
6. Ibid.
7. http://www.nj.gov/oag/newsreleases03/pr20031211a.html.
8. Adapted from Federal Trade Commission www.ftc.gov/idtheft.
9. Ibid.
10. Ibid.
11. http://www.fbi.gov/publications/financial/fcs_report2006/financial_crime_2006.htm.
12. Ibid.

CHAPTER 7

Analytic Tools and Audit Checklists

To exist is to change, to change is to mature, to mature is to go on creating oneself endlessly.

—HENRI BERGSON (1859–1941), FRENCH PHILOSOPHER

The role of the e-health auditor is to examine business processes and test the use of appropriate internal controls to ensure the integrity of e-health infrastructures. Auditors use analytics to break down information into data elements and extract basic principles to understand the interrelationships among those data elements and their impact on a specific task or subject. An effective e-health audit often requires analysis of programming components to develop algorithms and comprehend the manipulations and modifications of data that the algorithms process. Analytic tools are simply the technologies that drive the software and techniques that house the algorithms used to review a specific function or task. Auditors also typically use checklists to collect and analyze data. Examples of auditor checklists appear throughout this book.

Thus far, this book has covered industry applications of e-health data, including niche concepts such as clinical and financial case management. It has also covered the various types of algorithms that can be developed to manipulate or process data. The previous chapter focused on understanding the mechanics behind data-driven health decisions and the models for evaluating particular infrastructures. This chapter will focus on the analytic tools necessary to understand business processes.

Escalating healthcare costs continue to affect the entire marketplace from delivery to the financing of healthcare services. In our competitive capitalistic environment, which faces pressure for cost savings from both private and public entities, interest customarily focuses on improving the business process and the evolution and modification of effective platforms. Numerous academic institutions, professional associations, and audit techniques can provide auditors with the deep level of analytical understanding required to keep up with market demands.

The Institute of Internal Auditors (www.theiia.org) is a valuable resource and professional training organization for individuals who would like to expand their audit expertise and capabilities. Likewise, the Association of Certified Fraud Examiners (www.acfe.com) is a valuable resource for individuals who want to develop investigative skills to detect anomalies. Another organization that warrants recognition is the International Organization for Standardization (www.iso.org), in Geneva, Switzerland, which dedicates itself to developing standards for quality control. Its quality standards are recognized worldwide.

Auditors have used numerous techniques to review a business process. *Total quality management* (TQM) is an audit approach that relies on an interactive team to address issues to spur continuous improvement, whereas *benchmarking* compares business practices under review with best-in-show practice models and *quality audits* determine the best and worst practice activities. Auditors use *gap analysis* to understand specific problems and how to mitigate them and *process flow analysis* or *flowcharting* to illustrate operational components of a specific function. (Examples in this book are in flowchart format to illustrate general categories of business functions.) Statistical tools such as *control charts* visually separate variant occurrences from normal occurrences, and *cause-and-effect diagrams* map issues under review. For instance, *histograms* can facilitate the evaluation of the frequency with which a particular set of data elements appear within an activity. Auditors also use *run charts* to illustrate activity, trends, and variances over time. Another common approach to reviewing quality is the *six sigma* process, which emphasizes data-driven methodology to narrow issues under scope within a particular process review. Other general skill sets necessary to develop under a comprehensive audit curriculum include forecasting methods, project management techniques, business process analysis, inventory management techniques and concepts, marketing from a pricing and policy perspective, supply chain management concepts, and human resource management.

E-Health and Healthcare Business Processes

What is a business process and what does it involve? A business process is a systematic series of steps to achieve operational objectives and conclusion of a specific trade, service, or product. This chapter outlines business processes for each market player within the primary healthcare continuum and identifies impacting e-health initiatives. In formulating any business process, auditors should consider user expectations, available resources, and access to information.

Patient Business Process

Exhibit 7.1 illustrates the patient business process.

EXHIBIT 7.1   BUSINESS PROCESS: PATIENT

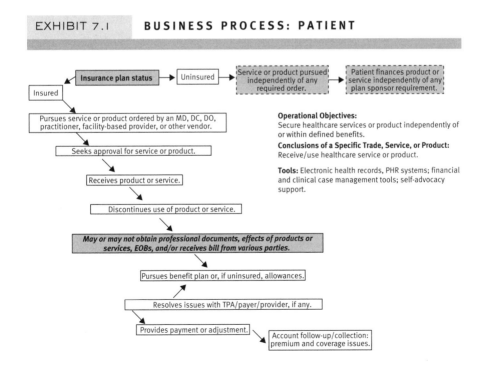

What types of expectations do patients have? Patients likely expect competent healthcare services and unbiased health recommendations, and, in an e-health environment, they may demand access to their health information whenever they need it.

What types of resources are available to provide services that meet patient expectations? Typically, patients interact with healthcare providers, payer utilization departments, and claims agents—a minimum of three different resources—when a healthcare episode does not encounter any setbacks. From the patient perspective, the pivotal point in the business process is whether a patient has insurance. (Note that the process is more involved for benefit program participants.)

What types of access to information are available to patients? Current market limitations include a lack of transparency of information and communication between the patient and all other market players within the healthcare continuum. Another important limitation is a lack of interoperable information that makes self-advocacy and the task of obtaining relevant patient information cumbersome. E-health initiatives attempt to create a fluid interoperable environment throughout the entire business process in which patient information is accessible during subsequent requests for service. Let's take a look at the following financial and clinical problems run into by patients.

Problem #1: Financial Case Management Advocacy

"Nora" was an 87-year-old widow. Her husband "Ethan," a Medicaid and Medicare recipient, had died in a nursing home. The nursing home was a Medicaid provider and received monthly payment of $1,250 from Medicaid. Nora and Ethan's children had been contributing supplemental payments of $1,444.60 per month.

Two years after Ethan's death, the nursing home hired a new billing agent who went through receivables and initiated billings on accounts in which agreed-on deductions had been made. It then initiated supplemental billing statements during the three-year period in which Ethan received services and filed a claim against Nora for $21,792 in additional charges.

Nora was aware of neither her own nor her deceased husband's rights and did not understand the concept of balance billing. A lack of transparent reimbursement rules further complicated matters. E-health's ability to create an interoperable environment for billing information among the provider, plan sponsor (Medicaid in this case), and the patient will help alleviate this type of confusion.

Problem #2: Clinical Case Management Advocacy

Recall "Dina" from Chapter 3, our 56-year-old female cancer patient who had never undergone surgery until her cancer diagnosis. Dina had initiated consultations with her family doctor, oncologist, surgeon, pain management specialist, rehabilitation expert, and radiation oncology expert. She received two second opinions and a series of diagnostic and laboratory tests. Each provider initiated his or her consultation and examination without the medical records accumulated from preceding providers, and, unfortunately, Dina ended up experiencing interoperative awakening.

A lack of real-time access to Dina's entire updated medical record caused providers to make assessments without complete information. E-health's ability to create an interoperable environment for health data will promote complete data-driven healthcare decisions that minimize potential for medical errors and provide optimal solutions.

PROVIDER BUSINESS PROCESS

Exhibit 7.2 illustrates the typical provider business process. The provider setting is split into two groups: the facilities where services are provided and the professionals who provide those services. It is especially important to recognize professionals who bill for their services independent of any facility fee to understand how providers generate fees. For example, a hospital will charge for facility use but will not charge for the nurse who took care of the patient or the pharmacist who prepared medications. The physician, however, acting as an outside consultant to the patient's care, bills for the diagnostic or procedural services provided.

E-health auditors must determine what e-infrastructures exist that enable providers to communicate internally and externally with other market players during the business process. *Registration* is a critical step in the provider business process. Auditors must determine how providers obtain registration information and how it connects with *third-party audits and*

EXHIBIT 7.2   BUSINESS PROCESS: PROVIDERS

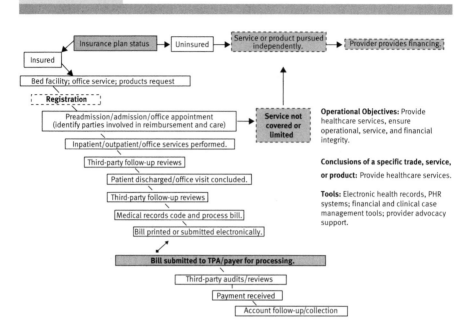

reviews and *account follow-up/collections*. For instance, how much of the process is still dependent on paper and left to convert into an electronic environment?

The provider setting still faces significant limitations to interoperability. The following provides examples of problems that occur due to ineffective implementation of electronic health record (EHR) systems and lack of interoperability.

Problem #1: Lack of Electronic Internal Controls

When a 300-bed hospital purchased an EHR system, it realized upon implementation that the functional tools for the operating system did not include user-tracking controls for hospital employees. An audit of patient and financial records indicated that the EHR preserved only the last entry into the system, resulting in an inability to track user changes, additions, modifications, or deletions of content. E-health's ability to create interoperability coupled with appropriate user internal controls will promote electronic data integrity.

Problem #2: Lack of Internal Controls with User Identity

When a 200-bed hospital purchased and implemented an EHR system, the patient-tracking tool installed could not correlate patient financial account numbers with their respective medical record numbers. An audit of the patients' medical record numbers and financial accounting record numbers indicated that the EHR programming did not take into account the attributes of the health data tracked by a medical record number and the financial data tracked by an account number. The result of this deficiency meant that a patient's laboratory would never correlate with the financial system's billing account number. To make matters worse, the system did not retrieve patients' unique medical record identifier numbers. Any time patients returned to the hospital, they were denoted as a new patient in the system.

The inability effectively to correlate medical record numbers with new account numbers and subsequent episodes of care resulted in "missing" patients within the system and nonsubmitted claims. When claims were submitted, they contained integrity issues, and the selection of diagnostic and procedural information raised the potential for misrepresentation of services rendered by the facility. A medical records department depends on health data to select appropriate diagnostic and procedure codes. When a disruption of aggregating information occurs, a hospital may make incorrect code decisions based on incomplete records. E-health's ability to create interoperability coupled with appropriate internal controls for patient identification from a clinical and financial perspective will promote data integrity of the health and financial information collected during an episode of care.

Problem #3: Lack of Internal Controls for Services Provided and Charged

When a 450-bed hospital purchased and implemented an EHR system, it did not program its charge master (a listing of services and products provided to the patient) with individual unique identifiers. An audit comparing patient final bills to patient medical records could not be completed because any tracking of services was compromised by generic numbers. The hospital therefore was unable to generate prior cost accounting reports by hospital department or post-discharge audit adjustments of over- and undercharges, or measure expenditures by disease category, preventing the evaluation of effective resource utilization. E-health's ability to create interoperability coupled with appropriate internal controls for individually identifiable service and product charges will be critical in maintaining financial integrity and disease management accountability.

PAYER BUSINESS PROCESS

Exhibit 7.3 illustrates the typical payer business process. Both insurance companies and TPAs process healthcare claims. Payer processes have a variety of questions for auditors to address: What type of electronic system is used to process claims? What contractual fee schedules for services and products exist within a network? Does an entity manage clinical data differently from financial data? Within an electronic claims environment, for what percentage of claims does an entity handle claims processing electronically? Does an entity still receive paper claims? It is also important to break down electronic handling of business processes. For example, a

EXHIBIT 7.3   BUSINESS PROCESS: PAYER, TPA, OR INSURANCE COMPANY

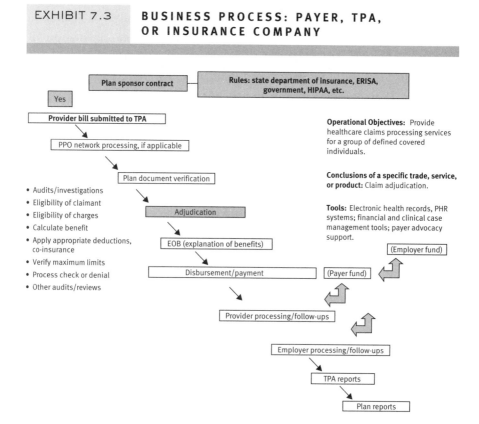

system that converts 10 manual steps into 10 electronic steps is likely not taking advantage of technology.

Auditors should furthermore ensure that appropriate communication and exchange of information among plan sponsors exists. TPAs often process claims on behalf of a third-party plan sponsor, and defined access to information and prevention of breaches are important parts of the business process.

The following questions might be asked on a payer audit assessment questionnaire:

- How many providers are under contract?
- What percentage of claims is paid within versus out of network?
- How are claims paid and processed?
- What management reports are used for tracking claims?
- What internal controls are in place to verify contractual guarantees?
- How can contractual terms be audited and/or corroborated?
- How are false claims investigated?
- What results have surfaced from previous audits or investigations?

E-health initiatives in the payer marketplace are predominately financial in nature, relating to processing and verifying claims. When a provider submits a claim form to a payer, the provider includes supporting documentation from a patient medical record. The market currently lacks the necessary structure to maintain complete files on individual patients. Providing the "minimum necessary" for claim verification is still the industry standard. One niche aspect in the payer environment considers results for when a patient releases a complete health record for consideration of benefits. It is unclear today what happens to records when a payer does not accept a patient for coverage. If a payer does accept a patient for coverage, how does the payer use those records in the future?

Some payers are beginning to offer some type of personal health record (PHR) system to their beneficiaries. These offerings are the first to provide a fluid electronic exchange of billing information. These PHRs include calendars to track health appointments and various sorts of health history repositories. Some of these PHRs even offer opportunities to scan in actual health records. A challenge facing payer PHRs, however, is consumer confidence in privacy. For example, will nonrelated health information be secured? In a payer PHR system, if a patient pursues non-covered health services, will privacy and access be controlled?

Following are some problems related to payer information issues.

Problem #1: Use and Loss of Health Information—Handling Subcontracted Vendors

National insurance carriers often use brokers to sell insurance coverage and enroll potential beneficiaries into a program by facilitating the enrollment application and obtaining health data. Therefore, brokers collect, store, handle, process, and transfer health information even though they do not typically evaluate any of it. What happens when a broker loses a file containing health information, and what internal controls ensure the integrity of enrollment processes? E-health's ability to create interoperability could create an e-health infrastructure for a secure enrollment process, eliminating the unnecessary handling of health information by brokers. Providing patients with direct electronic access to share health information could also provide a cost-effective solution.

Problem #2: Lack of Insurance—Processing Fraudulent Claims for Enrolled Beneficiaries

Eligibility verification is a traditional payer function coordinated with plan sponsors that now tends to be done electronically. People who do not hold health insurance may be able to persuade those who are covered to file fraudulent claims for their medications. When a TPA does not reconcile pharmacy benefit managers' medication information with health data, these fraudulent transactions may slip through the system unnoticed and compromise the integrity of the beneficiary file. E-health's ability to create interoperable disease management protocols and medication profiles will provide the optimal environment to ensure claim submission integrity. Interoperability will also help identify patient medication complications, thus preventing and minimizing the impact of medical errors.

PLAN SPONSOR BUSINESS PROCESS

The plan sponsor business process typically varies from one entity to the next. Plan sponsors fall into one of several different categories: self-insured nongovernmental employers subject to ERISA guidelines and provisions, government-sponsored programs such as Medicare and Medicaid subject to legislated mandates accompanied by Centers for Medicaid and Medicare (CMS) guidelines, and private insurance companies that sell insurance coverage. These private plans are subject to state department of insurance provisions and mandates. Auditors should determine what controls are in place to monitor access and use of this data. Exhibit 7.4 illustrates a basic plan sponsor business process guideline. Auditors should use it to flesh out a comprehensive list of activities when reviewing a particular plan sponsor.

Auditors can use the following checklist to help identify exchanges in e-health clinical and financial data within the plan sponsor business process:

- Identify parties involved in the benefit plan management by collecting signed and unsigned contracts. (Do not overlook subcontracted vendors.)
- Identify all fee schedules within each contract.
- Determine sources of data, access parameters, and how data is corroborated.
- Identify right-to-audit provisions and the access level allowed.

EXHIBIT 7.4   **BUSINESS PROCESS: PLAN SPONSOR**

Plan sponsor

Rules: state department of insurance, ERISA, legislation, HIPAA, etc.

Contract with TPA

Implement contracted terms: set up controls for monitoring terms.

Plan document verification/audit/monitoring

- Audits/investigations
- Eligibility of claimant
- Eligibility of charges
- Calculate benefit
- Apply appropriate deductions, co-insurance
- Verify maximum limits
- Process check or denial
- Verify TPA fees
- Verify subcontractor fees
- Conduct QA audits
- Verify internal controls
- Verify employee internal controls

Vendor audits

EOB (explanation of benefits)

Disbursement/payment

TPA processing/follow-ups

Employer processing/follow-ups

TPA reports

(Employer fund)

(Payer fund)

Operational Objectives: Provide defined healthcare benefits to a specified population.

Conclusions of a specific trade, service, or product: Ensure program integrity and compliance of benefit plan.

Tools: Electronic health records, PHR Systems; financial and clinical case management tools; employer advocacy support.

- Identify which monetary transactions cannot be audited or corroborated.
- Collect reports that demonstrate adjudication according to the plan document and the source of data that is used for the basis of decisions.
- Identify claims not paid according to plan.
- Identify source of plan information.
- Identify internal controls within the business process.

Plan sponsor e-health initiatives relate to the movement of beneficiary health and financial information. Plan sponsors are also initiating PHR offerings for their beneficiaries. Understanding the value of a particular PHR offering requires an evaluation of the objectives and relationships involved. For example, if an employer develops a PHR offering in tandem with a local hospital, how is information that is generated outside the hospital setting handled, and exactly what level of user content control will exist?

The following problems relate to plan sponsor information issues.

Problem #1: Employee Working Environments

Employers generally initiate periodic quality control reviews of working environments to ensure safety. Assessments often include documenting adverse employee symptoms. For example, hospitals routinely screen and monitor employees with infectious conditions. How is the integrity of the employee health file maintained while an employer tests for potential hazardous exposure? How does an employer ensure that disclosure of any health-related information does not impact an employee's work status or subsequent raises and/or promotions? E-health's ability to create interoperable health information will provide opportunities for large-scale analysis and development of effective safety, prevention, and mitigation standards.

Problem #2: Employer Increase in Healthcare Expenditures

When an employer discovers a significant increase in health expenditures, it will often audit the plan to analyze the source of the expense increase and identify opportunities for cost reduction. How is the integrity of the employee health file maintained while an employer evaluates expenses? If an audit identifies specific employees as high risk, how will the information be handled? How will the discovery impact their job status? Some employee wellness programs construct specific health goals and consequences. For example, if employees do not complete a smoking-cessation program, they are terminated. Health policies directly impacting employment status is a new concept, and the implications of such policies are currently being tested in the marketplace. E-health's ability to create interoperable health information will provide opportunities for large-scale analysis and to improve disease management and reduce plan sponsor costs.

THIRD-PARTY VENDOR BUSINESS PROCESS

Auditors should use traditional methodologies to understand process, movement of information, and operational and financial impact as a guide to review any type of third-party vendor. Because the list of types of third-party vendors is as diverse as it is long, this chapter addresses one specific niche third-party vendor: pharmacy benefit managers (PBMs). The costs associated with the use of prescription medications have been increasing annually, causing PBMs to grow into larger players within the healthcare continuum. An analysis of PBMs also demonstrates how an interoperable e-health environment can unite a fragmented business process. Exhibit 7.5 illustrates the PBM market continuum.

The PBM marketplace is comprised of very complex relationships among business functions and e-health communications. Numerous contracts exist among the market players, and not all are transparent. Exhibit 7.6 illustrates typical product and monetary movement within the PBM marketplace.

The PBM marketplace is also complex because additional flows of product and monetary information move through independent channels via other service entities. For example, the employer may have a PBM manage its prescription benefits. Employers pay for this service through their TPA. The PBM contracts the retail delivery of drugs to patients. In this scenario, the employer, the TPA, and the PBM never see what drug is actually given to the patient. In addition, they typically do not have audit access to test, sample, and/or verify what drug the patient actually

EXHIBIT 7.5   **PBM HEALTHCARE CONTINUUM**

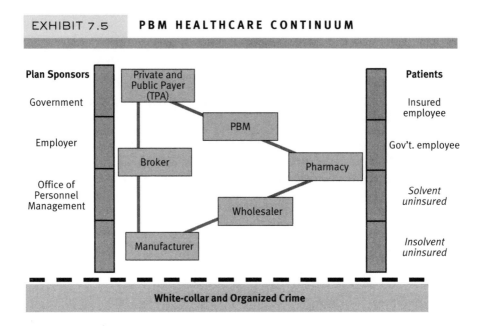

receives. Auditors also struggle to gain market access to follow the movement of one specific drug from manufacturer to patient consumption. E-health's ability to create interoperability in the PBM environment will ultimately unify its fragmented components. However, expect resistance from one or more of the market players noted in Exhibit 7.6 as the market evolves, because transparency will often provide clarity to all the monetary transactions that drive the relationships in this flowchart.

The following problem relates to a PBM information issue.

Problem: Increase in Pharmaceutical Expenditures

When an employer discovers a significant increase in healthcare expenditures and audits its plan, it may find that the increase in cost is due to pharmaceuticals. Employers may or may not have a direct contract with their PBM. The PBM relationship is typically managed by the employer's TPA; therefore, gaining appropriate access to retail dispensing activity and inventory documents to audit PBM transactions can prove difficult for employers. Furthermore, rebate programs set up between manufacturers and PBMs often provide disincentives for PBMs to substitute generic

EXHIBIT 7.6

PBM BUSINESS PROCESS

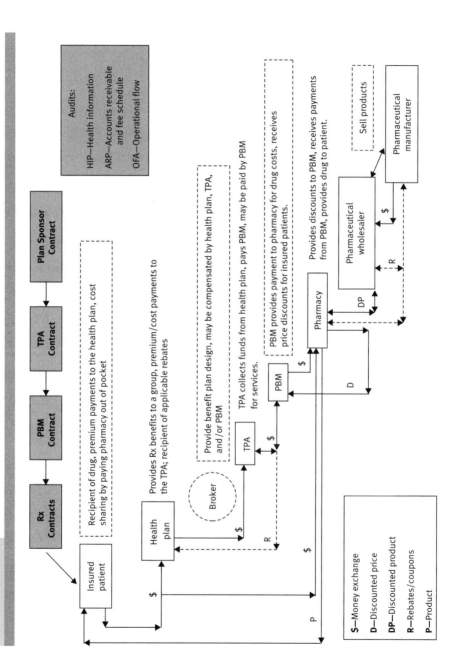

Audits:
HIP—Health information
ARP—Accounts receivable and fee schedule
OFA—Operational flow

Plan Sponsor Contract

TPA Contract

PBM Contract

Rx Contracts

Recipient of drug, premium payments to the health plan, cost sharing by paying pharmacy out of pocket

Provides Rx benefits to a group, premium/cost payments to the TPA; recipient of applicable rebates

Provide benefit plan design, may be compensated by health plan, TPA, and/or PBM

TPA collects funds from health plan, pays PBM, may be paid by PBM for services.

PBM provides payment to pharmacy for drug costs, receives price discounts for insured patients.

Provides discounts to PBM, receives payments from PBM, provides drug to patient.

Insured patient

Health plan

Broker

TPA

PBM

Pharmacy

Pharmaceutical wholesaler

Pharmaceutical manufacturer

Sell products

$—Money exchange
D—Discounted price
DP—Discounted product
R—Rebates/coupons
P—Product

medications for branded medications. E-health's ability to create interoperability and transparent financial transactions will help employers evaluate PBM activity more accurately.

Audit Implication Overview

This chapter explores market player business processes and the impact of e-health. To recap from the beginning, we first identified the critical entities in the delivery and payment processing of healthcare services in the primary healthcare continuum. We then looked at market factors that impact these entities in the secondary healthcare continuum. The information continuum identified the e-health infrastructure for these entities and market factors. We then explored data, how to manage data through algorithms, and its impact on the decision-making process. This chapter highlights the business processes in which data-driven decisions occur. The next chapter will review a sample of various electronic information infrastructures, and look at how data is currently shared and what the future holds.

CHAPTER 8

Electronic Health Records

When you're finished changing, you're finished.

—BENJAMIN FRANKLIN (1706–1790),
AMERICAN STATESMAN, SCIENTIST, AND PHILOSOPHER

On January 31, 2006, President George W. Bush declared, "We will make wider use of electronic records and other health information technology to help control costs and reduce dangerous medical errors." Today, numerous types of electronic infrastructures appear throughout the P-HCC and S-HCC. This chapter focuses on providers, who initiate health information, and payers, who receive health information through claims data.

CURRENT E-HEALTH OFFERINGS

Exhibits 8.1 and 8.2 demonstrate the vastness of e-health vendor offerings in the provider and payer marketplaces. Although the lists do not exhaust possible offering capabilities, they recognize the features and functions commonly advertised by vendors within respective market segments. Vendors tend to offer some combination of the features and functions listed. In addition, depending on the particular vendor, the technology behind each feature and function varies significantly.

The e-health provider offerings focus heavily on workflow and emphasize patient health records. Providers fundamentally treat patients and require aggregated comprehensive health information to do so effectively.

EXHIBIT 8.1   E-HEALTH PROVIDER OFFERINGS—PART I

Market Focus	Functions	Vendor Checklist
Providers	Billing	
	Blog activity—internal	
	Charge capture functions	
	Claims processing	
	Clearinghouse functions	
	Clinical decision-making tools	
	Clinical documentation	
	Coding rules and support tools	
	Compliance tools	
	Connectivity—device	
	Connectivity—internal	
	Connectivity—external	
	Contacts address book	
	Data storage solutions	
	Database technology solutions	
	Decision-support tools	
	Device connectivity	
	Document annotation	
	Documentation—procedures	
	Document management/imaging	
	X-rays, films, scans	
	Document template systems	
	Disease management tools	
	Educational tools—staff	
	Educational tools—patients	
	EHR acute care hospital	
	EHR specialty: ambulatory care	
	EHR specialty: cardiology	
	EHR specialty: chiropractic	
	EHR specialty: dermatology	
	EHR specialty: family medicine	
	EHR specialty: gastroenterology	

Market Focus	Functions	Vendor Checklist
	EHR specialty: hematology	
	EHR specialty: general surgery	
	EHR specialty: immunology	
	EHR specialty: internal medicine	
	EHR systems: medical specialties	

EXHIBIT 8.2 **E-HEALTH PROVIDER OFFERINGS—PART II**

Market Focus	Functions	Vendor Checklist
Providers	EHR specialty: neurology	
	EHR specialty: obstetrics/gyn	
	EHR specialty: oncology	
	EHR specialty: ophthalmology	
	EHR specialty: optometry	
	EHR specialty: otolaryngology	
	EHR specialty: orthopedics	
	EHR specialty: pediatrics	
	EHR specialty: podiatry	
	EHR specialty: primary care	
	EHR specialty: psychiatry	
	EHR specialty: radiology	
	EHR specialty: rheumatology	
	EHR specialty: surgery	
	EHR specialty: urology	
	EHR registration and discharge	
	Electronic refill requests and responses	
	Encounter forms	
	E-prescribing	
	Health information management services	
	Health-maintenance alert system	
	Health-adverse alert system	
	Health-reporting alert system	
	Health-rules alert system	

(Continued)

Market Focus	Functions	Vendor Checklist
	Integration/interface engines	
	Interactive voice response	
	Interoperability functions	
	Letter and form generation modules	
	Mark standards database engines	
	Marketing tools	
	Master patient indices (MPI)	
	Medical transcription sys/service	
	Multisite management	
	Networking systems (software)	
	Order entry applications	
	Outsourcing components	
	Patient portal support	
	Performance measurement support tools	
	Portability options	
	Practice communications management	
	Practice management solutions	
	Quality care indicators	
	Quality assurance tools	
	Revenue integrity tools	
	Scheduling	
	Secure instant messaging	
	Task and secure interoffice messaging tools	
	Transcription interface	
	Vital statistics	
	Workflow applications	
	Workflow automation	

The final deliverable of any provider healthcare service or product results in the generation of some type of *health notation* (a narrative describing some update on the patient, an assessment with new health information, and report finding). E-health offerings transfer these health notations into the electronic domain. Because each diagnostic category (e.g., oncology, neurology, etc.) possesses unique attributes, health notations vary, and vendors offer different e-health solutions for different diagnostic departments. Functionality such as *portability* and *connectivity* is critical to e-health offerings as the market moves toward an interoperable environment. Auditors can use Exhibits 8.1 and 8.2 as a checklist to assess and compare functional offerings between vendors.

Exhibits 8.3 and 8.4 demonstrate the market dynamics for e-health payer offerings. E-health payer offerings emphasize the systems requirements to process claims based on certain sets of rules. Validation of the service only requires the "minimum necessary" health information to confirm the contents of a claim. The need for comprehensive centralized patient records is not a direct workflow requirement. Payers tend to seek comprehensive patient records only when a need arises to investigate an individual patient or provider. Exhibit 8.3 and 8.4 list claims processing categories, such as Dental, Vision, Prescription, and Health. The business of processing claims does not readily require attention to subspecialty diagnostic categorization. Claims processing rather requires attention to the form in which a claim is received. For example, professionals submit healthcare claims on a *CMS* 1500 form. Providers submit facility based services on a *universal billing* form (UB04). Prescriptions and dentals also use their own type of claim form. Because payers rely on billing information contained on claim forms, they face significantly fewer issues than providers with respect to formatting communications of services rendered and respective fees.

Exhibit 8.5 presents a sample of e-health offering features and functions that provider and payer systems share (by subject, not necessarily in process).

The evolution of e-health is driven by market demands, business function requirements, and specific market player objectives. *Demands, requirements*, and *objectives* vary significantly among market players as evidenced between providers and payers. Therefore, it would be naive to expect the e-health infrastructures of these two market players to evolve in the same fashion. Providers thrive on centralized comprehensive information for the effective delivery of care; payers, in most cases, make do with the minimum necessary collection of health information to verify presenting claims. Providers and payers therefore will likely wrestle over market standards for e-health information standards.

EXHIBIT 8.3   E-HEALTH PAYER OFFERINGS—PART I

Market Focus	Functions	Vendor Checklist
Payers	Accounting integration	
	Actuarial reporting tools	
	Adjustor analysis tools	
	Adjustor management	
	Assign claims	
	Automated forms	
	Case management tools	
	Claims processing: dental	
	Claims processing: prescription	
	Claims processing: health	
	Claims processing: vision	
	Claims specialty: auto, life, P&C	
	Claims specialty: complex litigation	
	Claims specialty: excess coverage	
	Claims specialty: medical malpractice	
	Claims specialty: public entity	
	Claims specialty: workers' compensation	
	Claim and customer account history	
	Claim resolution tracking	
	COBRA administration	
	Coordination of benefits	
	Copays and deductible management	
	Cost analysis tools	
	CRM integration	
	Customer service integration capabilities	
	Custom user interface	
	Customizable fields	
	Customizable functionality	
	Data import/export	
	Data warehousing	
	Disability management tools	
	Documentation: case notes	
	Documentation: task management	
	Document imaging tools	
	Document repository	
	Diary and alert/alarm tools	

EXHIBIT 8.4   E-HEALTH PAYER OFFERINGS—PART II

Market Focus	Functions	Vendor Checklist
Payers	EDI capability	
	Edit tools	
	Electronic submission	
	HIPAA management (13)	
	Historical access retrieval system	
	Import and export functions	
	Legacy health systems	
	Emerging e-formats	
	Manual entry capability	
	Membership management	
	Mobile access	
	Modeling tools	
	Multicurrency and language	
	Multiple benefit programs support	
	Payment processing tools	
	Payer management	
	Policy management	
	Portability tools	
	Provider credentialing	
	Regulatory compliance management	
	Reporting capabilities	
	Customizable reporting	
	Rules-based adjudication	
	Consumer-driven	
	Federal employee products	
	HMO and PPO	
	Indemnity	
	Medicare/Medicaid	
	Premium billing	
	Self-insured management	
	Status tools	
	Turnkey tools	
	Validation tools	
	Workflow management	

EXHIBIT 8.5	SAMPLE LISTING OF SHARED VENDORS' FUNCTIONAL OFFERINGS

Provider	Payer
Accounting integration	Accounting integration
Billing	Claims processing: dental
Claims processing	Claims processing: prescription
	Claims processing: health
	Claims processing: vision
	Claims specialty: auto, life, P&C
	Claims specialty: complex litigation
	Claims specialty: excess coverage
	Claims specialty: medical malpractice
	Claims specialty: public entity
	Claims specialty: workers' compensation
	Claim and customer account history
	Claim resolution tracking
Clearinghouse functions	Data import/export
	Payment processing tools
Clinical documentation	Documentation: case notes
Portability options	Portability tools
Workflow applications	Workflow applications
Workflow automation	Workflow automation
Workflow management	Workflow management

When interviewing prospective e-health vendors, determine which features and functions are included in their electronic health system. The omission of certain categories can provide a great deal of insight into how well developed or versed a particular vendor is. More important, the market is going to change; if a vendor gives any signals that it has finished a complete comprehensive product for the ages, then take caution. Choosing a vendor that does not continue to adapt to the market will require an organization essentially to start over when the product becomes outdated or obsolete.

MARKET EVOLUTION

The healthcare industry desperately needs more commonality and transparency. The current universal billing form generated by the National Uniform Billing Committee (NUBC) facilitates claims developed because of the administrative simplification initiatives outlined in the Health Insurance Portability and Accountability Act (HIPAA) of 1996.[1] Exhibit 8.6 lists a sample of common transparent data elements that providers exchange with payers to share information in a consistent manner. Exhibit 8.7 lists the remaining data elements. Overall, 81 categories of information have been standardized. In comparison with a medical record on an individual patient, the number of elements to be defined would be in the thousands.

A similar list of shared fundamental data elements exists for processing professional fees. Laboratory result names have also experienced some kind of gentrification standards to facilitate clear communication. Initial laboratory result communication standards did not include recommendations for the name of the services ordered or the lab result values but simply focused on the standardization of the result names.[2] Exhibit 8.8 illustrates operational components for which commonality standards could be defined. Laboratory services fit into the category within the shaded box.

Exhibit 8.9 isolates the inpatient business process category that is found midstream in the provider business process (Exhibit 8.8) and illustrates key operational components in greater detail.

Each operational component within each business process requires a specific market standard if healthcare is to achieve true interoperability. Every hospital has a charge master that numerically lists all products and services that can be provided to patients, including the services identified in Exhibit 8.9. Charge masters can easily have 8,000 individual charge items, and each individual charge item can easily have up to 50 data elements documented to reflect service. Auditors should recognize each individual subcomponent. As illustrated in Exhibit 8.9, inpatient services break down into another 11 categories with 56 additional sublayers. The following is a list of other processes auditors need to consider to develop a complete picture of data element fields:

- Selection of room and board
- Provision of office services preadmission

EXHIBIT 8.6 **UB04 DATA CLAIM ELEMENTS: FIRST 41 STANDARDIZED DATA ELEMENTS**

Box #	Description
1	Facility name, address and phone number
2	Facility pay-to name and address
3a	Patient control# (patient account#) no change
3b	Medical record # (UB92 box 23)
4	Type of bill
5	Federal tax number
6	Statement covers period—from/through
7	Covered days
8a	Patient ID
8b	Patient name (UB92 box 12)
9a, 9b, 9c, 9d	Patient address, city, ZIP code, state (UB92 box 13)
10	Lifetime reserve days
11	Unlabeled
12	Patient name
13	Patient address
14	Patient birthdate
15	Patient sex
16	Patient marital status
17	Admission date
18	Admission hour
19	Type of admission/visit
20	Source of admission
21	Discharge hour
22	Patient status/discharge code
23	Medical record number
24–30	Condition codes
29	Accident state (new field)
31	Unlabeled
32–35	Occurrence code/date
39–41	Value codes

EXHIBIT 8.7

UB04 DATA CLAIM ELEMENTS: REMAINING STANDARDIZED DATA ELEMENTS

Box #	Description
42	Revenue code and line-level details
43	Revenue code description
44	HCPCS/rates/HIPPS rate codes
45	Service date creation date
46	Units of service
47	Total charges
48	Noncovered charges
49	Unlabeled
50	Payer name primary, secondary, tertiary
51	Health plan ID
52	Release of information primary secondary tertiary
53	Assignment of benefits primary secondary tertiary
54	Prior payments primary secondary tertiary
55	Estimated amount due primary secondary tertiary
56	National provider identifier (NPI)
57	Other physician ID primary secondary tertiary
58	Insured name primary secondary tertiary
59	Patient's relationship primary secondary tertiary
60	Insured unique ID primary secondary tertiary
61	Insured group name primary secondary tertiary
62	Insured groups number primary secondary tertiary
63	Treatment authorization code primary secondary tertiary
64	Document control number
65	Employer name primary secondary tertiary
66	DX qualifier
67	Diagnosis
68	Unlabeled
69	Admit diagnosis
70	Patient reason for visit
71	PPS code
72	External cause of injury
74a–e	Principal procedure code
75	Unlabeled
76	Attending—NPI/qual/ID
77	Operating—NPI/qual/ID
78	Other ID
79	Other ID
80	Remarks
81	Code to code field

EXHIBIT 8.8

BUSINESS PROCESS: PROVIDER FACILITY—GLOBAL CATEGORY OF OPERATIONS

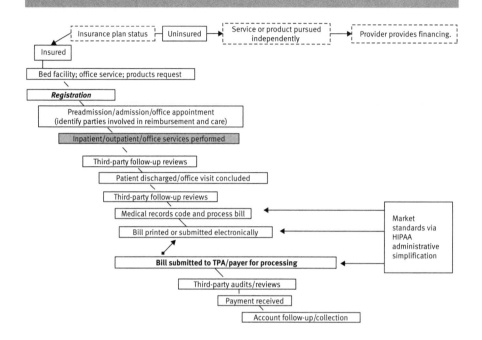

EXHIBIT 8.9

BUSINESS FOCUS: INPATIENT ACUTE CARE FACILITY

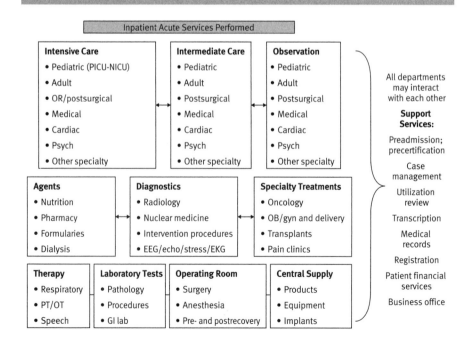

- Products request
- Registration
- Payer certification
- Preadmission
- Admission
- Office appointment
- Inpatient activity
- Outpatient activity
- Office service activity
- Third-party follow-up reviews
- Patient discharged
- Office visit concluded
- Medical records assembly
- Code of procedures
- Bill preparation
- Bill submission
- Bill pending status
- Payment received
- Account follow-up
- Collection

Today, these items, in whole or in part, may be communicated from one facility to another; however, the format and description of what is exchanged varies considerably. Common concerns affecting the development of market standards are the cost and availability of proven technology, stakeholders reaching agreement on standard content, and, most of all, the resulting transparency of monetary transactions.

E-HEALTH CONTENT STANDARDS

The examples discussed in the previous section focus on format and structure of electronic function offerings with two examples of standardized communications of billing data such as the UB04 form. Another area of the market to watch out for includes specific standards on clinical record content. One example includes the efforts of an organization started in 2003 known as Continuity of Care Record (CCR) standards.[3] Any auditor involved in analyzing or testing internal controls in the collection, organization, and movement of health data should monitor the developments of this organization.

The organization describes a sample of data objects that should be included in a CCR transaction between one provider and another in their respective patient record. The three components include the "header" of the electronic file; the "body," which is the content of the transmission; and the "footer," which describes authorship. The content for the header includes:

- Patient
- To
- From
- Purpose
- Date

The content for the body include:

- Adverse Directives
- Alerts
- Encounters
- Family History
- Functional Status
- Insurance
- Immunizations
- Medications
- Medical Equipment
- Plan of Care
- Problems
- Providers
- Results
- Social History
- Support
- Vital Signs

The content for the footer include:
- Actors
- Comments
- Signatures

The universal billing committee provided consistent market structure for all providers to submit billing data in the same format. Conceptually this organization is moving in the same direction by initiating content standards. The CCR standards target continuity of care and patient safety via the communication of core data elements via electronic transmissions. This cannot be done without setting standards for the organization of the content of health information.

E-HEALTH OFFERING VULNERABILITIES

Healthcare's most significant vulnerability as it markets into an e-health environment (putting aside the well-documented concerns over security and privacy) is ensuring that the vendor offerings actually perform as advertised. Many references and consultants are available to help facilitate e-health initiatives. It is important to establish a team that has operational understanding and know-how of each business process. Before a conversion to a new e-health system takes place, it is important to prepare backup plans for functions that appear not to work. Many entities have experienced pain because of provisions overlooked during the design of the e-health infrastructure. In addition to being a burden on staff, the cost of corrections can easily reach the seven- and eight-figure range.

The following case study presents what can and did go wrong during a system conversion.

CASE STUDY	AUDIT ASSESSMENT OF POST-CONVERSION EHR IMPLEMENTATION ISSUES— "THE SYSTEM IS NOT WORKING"

SUMMARY

A hospital's electronic health record (EHR) system experienced significant functionality issues in the following departments:

- Admissions
- Patient Billing Financial Services
- Collection Accounts Receivable
- Central Services Inventory Control
- Health Info Management (Medical Records)
- Insurance Verification
- Management

Over a period of 14 months, the listed departments remained nonfunctional, resulting in a "no-confidence level" by the hospital in its ability to generate and submit accurate patient claims. The dysfunction noted in the audit resulted in significant revenue and labor damages reaching multimillion-dollar figures. After significant revenue losses and compliance exposure, the hospital's CEO made a determination to discontinue EHR services. It was less expensive for the hospital to start over with an entirely new system than to fix problems with the current one.

Audit Activity

The following items were reviewed and analyzed for preparation to mitigate nonfunctional attributes:

- Operational analysis of the request for proposal (RFP):
  - Analysis of items categorized as "must have," "highly desirable," and "desirable"
  - Analysis of manual versus automatic functions
- Impact of attempted implementation
- Review of business office functions
- Design/implementation of employee interviews
- Impact of damage to the hospital
- Analysis of fluctuations in hospital revenues
- Analysis of fluctuations in census data
- Analysis of compliance and revenue impact
- Analysis of inefficiency impact
- Analysis of labor impact
- Financial damages

Data Profile 1: Contracted Functions

The EHR vendor contract pertained to 1,012 different hospital business functions in 27 different departments. Each function was assessed a priority level. Within each department listed in Exhibit 8.A, the vendor contract provided for items that were categorized as (1) Desirable, (2) Highly Desirable, (3) Must Have.

Exhibit 8.B provides a sample listing of "must-have" contracted items that the EHR vendor indicated it could already accommodate within the admissions department.

Exhibit 8.B illustrates the format in which the information was organized in an auditor worksheet. The first audit objective was to identify what functions were actually implemented. The

EXHIBIT 8.A **HOSPITAL DEPARTMENTS WITH EHR FUNCTIONS PROPOSED**

#	Hospital Department	#	Hospital Department
1	Admissions	15	Laboratory
2	Billing Patient Financial Services	16	Management
3	Collections Accounts Receivable	17	Marketing
4	Accounts Payable	18	Medical Staff Coordination
5	Case Management	19	Neurology (EKG, EMG, EEG)
6	Central Services Inventory Control	20	Nursing Order Entry
7	Communications	21	Payroll
8	Education Patient	22	Pharmacy
9	Emergency Room	23	Physical Therapy
10	General Ledger	24	Podiatry
11	Golden Clinic Kedzie Ave.	25	Radiology
12	Health Info Management (Med Rec)	26	Renal Dialysis
13	Information Systems	27	General
14	Insurance Verification		

EXHIBIT 8.B **EHR ADMISSIONS FUNCTIONS**

#	Function	Vendor Responsible	Priority	Implemented	Manual/Auto
1	Supports inpatient and outpatient registrations, including emergency room	Yes	3	Yes	Manual
2	Supports online ability to manually add, edit, or delete inpatient and locations: * Business—admitting * Emergency room—admitting * #1 Clinic	Yes	3	Yes	Manual
3	When adding a new patient registration, the system should default the discharge date to be the same as the admission date if the admitting disposition is outpatient.	Yes	3	No	Manual
18	The admissions, pharmacy, order entry, and billing functions should use the Physician Master List for validation purposes.	Yes	3	No	
19	Provide security that only the medical staff coordinator or other authorized personnel may add or edit physicians on the Physician Master List.	Yes	3	No	
20	Keep audit trail of who originally created the physician record and when.	Yes	3	No	

next objective was to determine if the function required manual user activity. Later analysis determined the impact on operations, financials, and compliance for each department in the hospital. Gathering this data is an extensive and time-consuming process.

The EHR vendor listed 69 total functions in its offering for admissions. The hospital rated the priority of the functions. The plan and contract categorized 55 of the 69 functions as "must-have functions." "Highly desirable functions" totaled 5 and "desirable functions" totaled 7 of the 69. Two items were not categorized. The audit within admissions found that the EHR vendor implemented 36 functions; 33 items were not installed or demonstrated no capability. Out of all of the functions implemented, 9 resulted in automation and 27 still required manual user activity to complete the function. The remaining functions did not work in any capacity.

Exhibit 8.B illustrates audit results for 6 of the 69 functions reviewed within the admissions department. When a specific function did not work at all, the level of risk was assessed. Functions #18 and #19 were critical nonfunctioning items. Imagine being a patient in a facility that did not have the ability to verify the legitimacy of a physician prescribing medications. Function #20 was also very significant. The EHR system implemented did not have an audit trail function to track entries. This issue surfaced in every department in which the EHR system was implemented. As a result, no security existed to protect or monitor user activity.

DATA PROFILE 2: VENDOR STATEMENTS

The audit included a review of the narrative presentation of the contract and proposal. A few key statements were pulled from the narratives. The audit determined that the EHR vendor misrepresented its experience and implementation functions. The audit corroborates neither experience reported nor functions expressed in the capability statement.

Executive Summary Statements

"Our proposed application suite is an integrated solution that will meet the needs of the facility for years to come."

"The basis of our approach is centered on our approach of utilizing an enterprise-wide Master Patient Index across the Hospitals XXX Continuum of Care."

"As with most initiatives, the Hospital's XXX Specifications will require only minor modifications for compliance. Flexibility is a key ingredient to our software. Our ability to personalize your software, while not making any changes to the source code, allows the Hospital's XXX to significantly increase their return on investment."

". . . our implementation process is also a well tuned and proven methodology that has worked very successfully for our 200 customers over the last 21 years."

The RFP noted the following comments regarding the EHR vendor:

Company Background Statements

"Develops powerful, integrated software applications for all types of healthcare facilities including hospitals, nursing homes, surgery centers, home health agencies, clinics and medical facilities."

"Headquartered in XXXX, with regional offices in X other states."

DATA PROFILE 3: ANALYSIS OF BUSINESS FUNCTIONS BY HOSPITAL DEPARTMENT

The proposal included a listing of functions to be delivered. Each function had a rating associated and designated by the provider. For example, the rating "must-have" indicated that this was a mandatory requirement of the system and the vendor responding that they in fact do have the function available. The list continues with two other designations of "highly desirable" and "desirable" with respect to availability by the vendor in addition to the priority ranking of the function. The must-have items were mandatory functions requested by the provider and committed to by the vendor. The following list is a summary breakdown of the number of functions that fell into each category.

- 1,015 functions were presented in e-health vendor proposal.
- 830 (82%) functions were designated by hospital as "must have."
- 114 (11%) functions were designated by hospital as "highly desirable."
- 55 (5%) functions were designated by hospital as "desirable."

Exhibit 8.C provides a detailed listing by department and the assignment category for each area. In the audit process, it was

EXHIBIT 8.C   **PROFILE OF EHR PRIORITY LEVEL BY DEPARTMENT**

Contract Analysis: Identification of Activity by Defined Priority Level

ID	Department	None	Desirable Priority 1	Highly Desirable Priority 2	Must Have Priority 3	Count of Function	% of Total
1	Admissions	2	7	5	55	69	6.8%
2	Billing Patient Financial Services	0	4	1	81	86	8.5%
3	Collections Accounts Receivable	0	0	5	29	34	3.35%
4	Accounts Payable	0	0	19	0	19	1.87%
5	Case Management	0	0	0	37	37	3.65%
6	Central Services Inventory Control	1	0	5	12	18	1.77%
7	Communications	0	2	0	0	2	0.20%
8	Education Patient	0	10	0	0	10	0.99%
9	Emergency Room	0	0	0	21	21	2.07%
10	General Ledger	0	0	14	0	14	1.38%
11	Clinic #1	5	0	0	20	25	2.46%
12	Health Info Management	0	1	64	35	100	9.85%
13	Information Systems	0	0	0	20	20	1.97%
14	Insurance Verification	0	0	0	6	6	0.59%
15	Laboratory	0	0	0	47	47	4.63%
16	Management	7	0	0	98	105	10.34%
17	Marketing	0	12	0	0	12	1.18%
18	Medical Staff Coordinator	1	0	0	18	19	1.87%
19	Neurology (EKG, EMG, EEG)	0	1	0	42	43	4.24%
20	Nursing Order Entry	0	8	0	69	77	7.59%
21	Payroll	0	9	0	0	9	0.89%
22	Pharmacy	0	0	1	66	67	6.60%
23	Physical Therapy	0	0	0	41	41	4.04%
24	Podiatry	0	1	0	42	43	4.24%
25	Radiology	0	0	0	39	39	3.84%
26	Renal Dialysis	0	0	0	38	38	3.74%
27	General	0	0	0	14	14	1.38%
		16	55	114	830	1015	

important to utilize the original offering of the EHR system in order to compare what was actually provided post-implementation.

DATA PROFILE 4: AUDIT RESULT OF FUNCTIONALITY

Please note that overall, 55 percent of the functions were never implemented because of significant issues with the ability to resolve nonworking functions listed under "department" in Exhibit 8.C. The system failed in very critical operating areas of the hospital. The first department listed is "admissions." The issues noted included the inability to track the patient from the time of admission and forward along with any financial management of the care provided. As shown in Exhibit 8.D, the audit of the items implemented noted the following statistics:

- 19 percent of the functions overall did not work.
- 51 percent of the admission functions did not work.

EXHIBIT 8.D   AUDIT ASSESSMENT OF FUNCTIONS
               IMPLEMENTED

Audit Assessment of Functions and Implementation Response

ID	Department	Working Yes	Working No	Count of Function	% of Total as Yes	% of Total as No
1	Admissions	34	35	69	49.3%	51%
2	Billing Patient Financial Services	51	35	86	59.3%	41%
3	Collections Accounts Receivable	20	14	34	58.82%	41%
4	Accounts Payable	7	12	19	36.84%	63%
5	Case Management	37	0	37	100.00%	0%
6	Central Services Inventory Control	18	0	18	100.00%	0%
7	Communications	2	0	2	100.00%	0%
8	Education Patient	10	0	10	100.00%	0%
9	Emergency Room	21	0	21	100.00%	0%
10	General Ledger	4	10	14	28.57%	71%
11	Clinic #1	19	6	25	76.00%	24%
12	Health Info Management	99	1	100	99.00%	1%
13	Information Systems	3	17	20	15.00%	85%
14	Insurance Verification	6	0	6	100.00%	0%
15	Laboratory	47	0	47	100.00%	0%
16	Management	87	18	105	82.86%	17%
17	Marketing	12	0	12	100.00%	0%
18	Medical Staff Coordinator	19	0	19	100.00%	0%
19	Neurology (EKG, EMG, EEG)	43	0	43	100.00%	0%
20	Nursing Order Entry	77	0	77	100.00%	0%
21	Payroll	9	0	9	100.00%	0%
22	Pharmacy	33	34	67	49.25%	51%
23	Physical Therapy	41	0	41	100.00%	0%
24	Podiatry	43	0	43	100.00%	0%
25	Radiology	39	0	39	100.00%	0%
26	Renal Dialysis	38	0	38	100.00%	0%
27	General	4	10	14	28.57%	71%
		823	192	1015	81%	19%

- 41 percent of the billing and patient financial services functions did not work.
- 63 percent of the accounts payable functions did not work.

An interview matrix was created to consistently evaluate the employee response to the implemented functions. Some of the functions had two or more issues identified. The results of those interviews are noted in Exhibit 8.E.

Exhibit 8.F is a subcategory of items designated in the contract as "must have."

Exhibit 8.G breaks down the response by category "highly desirable."

Exhibit 8.H breaks down the response by category "desirable."

EXHIBIT 8.E   **CATEGORY OF ISSUES IDENTIFIED DURING EMPLOYEE INTERVIEWS**

Category of Issues Identified During Employee Interviews			
Issue Found	Issue Description	# of Business Functions with This Issue	% of Business Functions with This Issue
No Issues	No issues identified N/A	57	5.64%
Issue 1	Never implemented due to contract issues	563	55.74%
Issue 2	Electronic record never provided	255	25.25%
Issue 3	Not part of AHN system	18	1.78%
Issue 4	Never reviewed, tested, trained	232	22.97%
Issue 5	Interface issues	206	20.40%
Issue 6	No audit trail	406	40.20%
Issue 7	Never worked	108	10.69%
Issue 8	Data integrity	386	38.22%

Total Activity	2231
Total with No Issue	−57
Total Never Implemented	−563
Total Activity with Issues	1611 72.21%

EXHIBIT 8.F   **ANALYSIS OF LEVEL 3—MUST HAVE CRITERIA**

Analysis of Level 3 Must Have Criteria				
Priority	Type of Issue	Description	# of Functions	%
3	No Issue	Functions with no issued identified*	36	1.98%
3	Issue 1	Never implemented due to contract issues*	448	24.64%
3	Issue 2	Electronic record never provided	179	9.85%
3	Issue 3	Not part of AHN system	0	0.00%
3	Issue 4	Never reviewed, tested, trained	177	9.74%
3	Issue 5	Interface issues	191	10.51%
3	Issue 6	No audit trail	356	19.58%
3	Issue 7	Never worked	95	5.23%
3	Issue 8	Data integrity	336	18.48%

Total		1818
No Issue		−36
Issue 1		−448
Total with Issues		1334 73.38%

Level 3 Functions	Total RFP Functions	827
Average	Average number of issues per level 3	1.61

Exhibit 8.I illustrates that 83 percent of the issues and unresolved problems fell into the "must have" category.

In addition, the functions' status as automatic versus manual attribute was also evaluated. Exhibit 8.J illustrates that of the implemented EHR functions, 35.57 percent are classified as manual. *Manual* is defined as an employee having to do the same number of "paper steps" as "computer steps." Only 8.97 percent

EXHIBIT 8.G   ANALYSIS OF LEVEL 2—HIGHLY DESIRABLE CRITERIA

Priority	Type of Issue	Description	# of Functions	%
2	No Issue	Functions with no issued identified*	21	8.20%
2	Issue 1	Never implemented due to contract issues*	64	25.00%
2	Issue 2	Electronic record never provided	59	23.05%
2	Issue 3	Not part of AHN system	18	7.03%
2	Issue 4	Never reviewed, tested, trained	26	10.16%
2	Issue 5	Interface issues	4	1.56%
2	Issue 6	No audit trail	29	11.33%
2	Issue 7	Never worked	6	2.34%
2	Issue 8	Data integrity	29	11.33%

Analysis of Level 2 Highly Desirable Criteria

Total Items 256
No Issue −21
Issue 1 −64
Total with Issues 171   66.80%

Total RFP Functions 114
Average number of issues per level 2 1.50

EXHIBIT 8.H   ANALYSIS OF LEVEL 1—DESIRABLE CRITERIA

Priority	Type of Issue	Description	# of Functions	%
1	No Issue	Functions with no issued identified*	0	0.00%
1	Issue 1	Never implemented due to contract issues*	43	34.96%
1	Issue 2	Electronic record never provided	17	13.82%
1	Issue 3	Not part of AHN system	0	0.00%
1	Issue 4	Never reviewed, tested, trained	22	17.89%
1	Issue 5	Interface issues	10	8.13%
1	Issue 6	No audit trail	13	10.57%
1	Issue 7	Never worked	5	4.07%
1	Issue 8	Data integrity	13	10.57%

Analysis of Level 1 Desirable Criteria

Total Items 123
No Issue 0
Issue 1 −43
Total with Issues 80   65.04%

Total RFP Functions 55
Average number of issues per level 1 1.45

of the functions provided automated execution. Finally, 55.47 percent of the functions remained unchanged. Therefore, the progress of efficiency within the EHR system was not realized.

Exhibit 8.K illustrates impact by job function. The review did not address all of management (or senior management) who

EXHIBIT 8.I   DISTRIBUTION OF ISSUES IDENTIFIED BY
LEVEL CRITERIA

Distribution of Issues Identified by Level Criteria			
Level	Description	# of Issues	%
3	Must Have	1782	83.27%
2	Highly Desirable	235	10.98%
1	Desirable	123	5.75%
	Total	2140	

EXHIBIT 8.J   DATA PROFILE: AUTOMATIC VERSUS MANUAL
FUNCTIONS

Analysis of the Quantity of Functions Implemented Manual versus Automatic		
Function	# of Functions	% of Total
Manual	361	35.57%
Automatic	91	8.97%
Unchanged	563	55.47%
Total	1015	

did involve themselves in resolving many of the issues that are raised by the audit, including that the EHR system generated incorrect claim information. The focus of the "jobs" was on those positions that are on the front line. The impact is noted in the last column. The function of admitting the patient into the system is critical from a compliance and financial integrity perspective. The initial designation of the patient is what determines the system's ability to track the electronic information of that patient. If the patient is mislabeled, numerous issues, from patient safety to financial integrity, are compromised.

When an error or malfunction in the EHR software occurred, employees who held the job functions listed in Exhibit 8.K faced the resulting problems during each patient care episode. The impact was significant unanticipated labor costs. Exhibit 8.L provides additional critical highlights from the audit. The Diagnosis-Related Group (DRG) system, which is dependent on health information and updated coding information, is the reimbursement formula for how the hospital gets paid from Medicare.

EXHIBIT 8.K

DATA PROFILE: JOB IMPACT

Example #1:

Job Function	Department	RFP#	Description	Impact
Registration	Admissions	10	Enforces Medicare benefits prequalification via ABN for all Medicare outpatients during the registration process.	Patient admitted without proper registration
Utilization Review				Will have to respond to denials or other issue as a result of improper registration
Medical Coder				Should be able to code
Biller				Will have to resubmit bills after any corrections
Utilization Review				May have to get involved with errors, communicate with registration, HIM, collector
Collector				Will have to communicate with above parties
Registration/Patient Accts Director				May get involved with any party above Provide approval for writeoffs and/or adjustments

Job Function	Department	RFP#	Description	Impact
Registration	Admissions	7	Batch interface	Data integrity & manual changes
Utilization Review				Data integrity & manual changes
Medical Coder				Data integrity & manual changes Potential for lost records
Biller				Data integrity & manual changes Potential for lost records
Utilization Review				Data integrity & manual changes Follow-up payer calls Follow-up SH dept calls
Collector				Data integrity & manual changes Follow-up payer calls Follow-up SH dept calls
Registration/Patient Accts Director				Data integrity & manual changes Follow-up payer calls Follow-up SH dept calls Management of lost records and or writeoff decisions

EXHIBIT 8.L DIAGNOSIS-RELAXED GROUP-IMPACT

Example #2

Job Function	Department	RFP#	Description	Impact
Registration	Billing Patient Financial Services	60	Supports ability to manually update the Medicare DRG Reimbursements table. This must include the ability to add, edit, and inactivate DRG codes, descriptions, the Basic DRG dollars, allowance, Medicare DRG weighting and disproportionate share dollars.	Patient will be registered properly if all items under admissions were working properly.
Utilization Review			Supports ability to manually update the Medicaid (Public Aid) DRG Reimbursements table. This must include the ability to add, edit, and inactivate DRG codes, descriptions, the Basic DRG dollars, allowance, Medicaid DRG weighting and daily disproportionate.	Data integrity manual changes / Follow-up payer calls / Follow-up SH dept calls / OIG compliance issues / Work with management
		61	Supports ability to manually update the Medicaid (Public Aid) DRG Reimbursements table. This must include the ability to add, edit, and inactivate DRG codes, descriptions, the Basic DRG dollars, allowance, Medicaid DRG weighting and daily disproportionate.	
Medical Coder				Data integrity manual changes / Follow-up payer calls / Follow-up SH dept calls / OIG compliance issues / Work with management
Biller				If errors not caught, incorrect bills will be sent
Utilization Review				Follow-up as above if problem unresolved after discharge
Collector				Data integrity manual changes / OIG issues in pursuing collections on bills incorrectly submitted
Registration/Patient Accts Director				In addition to above, CEO involvement / Significant risk exposure for false claims

If this is not done correctly, the hospital could face significant compliance repercussions. The system's malfunction in this area placed the hospital in a vulnerable position.

Errors that occur while the patient is still in-house result in inefficiency, increased expenditures, and lost revenue. Once the patient is discharged and a bill leaves the hospital, the hospital faces increased exposure to compliance and potential false claim issues with both public and private payers.

Exhibit 8.M illustrates the impact within the hospital's operational flow from a revenue and compliance perspective. Exhibit 8.N is the key to the issues identified within Exhibit 8.M. I found issue #6 very significant since, at minimum, when an error was identified and/or corrected, the EHR system was unable to identify which user was involved.

EXHIBIT 8.M **DATA PROFILE: IMPACT ON COMPLIANCE AND REVENUE**

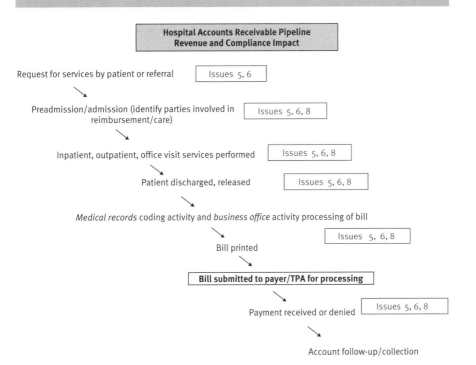

Hospital Accounts Receivable Pipeline Revenue and Compliance Impact

Request for services by patient or referral   Issues 5, 6

Preadmission/admission (identify parties involved in reimbursement/care)   Issues 5, 6, 8

Inpatient, outpatient, office visit services performed   Issues 5, 6, 8

Patient discharged, released   Issues 5, 6, 8

Medical records coding activity and *business office* activity processing of bill

Bill printed   Issues 5, 6, 8

Bill submitted to payer/TPA for processing

Payment received or denied   Issues 5, 6, 8

Account follow-up/collection

EXHIBIT 8.N   **KEY TO ISSUES IN EXHIBIT 8.M**

Issue Found	Issue Description
Issue 1	Never implemented due to contract issues
Issue 2	EHR system never provided
Issue 3	Not part of vendor system
Issue 4	Never reviewed, tested, trained
Issue 5	Interface issues
Issue 6	No audit trail
Issue 7	Never worked
Issue 8	Data integrity

An audit of the EHR system's impact on compliance and revenue revealed the following audit integrity issues impacting the representation of accurate revenue postings:

- Medicare Bad Debt Report requirement for CMS/Medicare.
- Inpatient and Outpatient IHCCCC Reporting for State was compromised.
- Medicare benefits prequalification screening via ABN (advanced beneficiary notice) for all outpatients, at registration.
- Provide same screening activity for all other payers.
- Interface issues.

The resulting nonfunctional operations along with the compromised functional areas that were implemented created additional labor hours to determine and correct problems. As a result, the audit included a measurement of efficiency issues. Exhibit 8.O illustrates the areas that were compromised, and Exhibit 8.P shows the key to efficiency issues.

An audit of the EHR system's impact on operations efficiency revealed the following audit integrity issues that resulted in manual processes (i.e., electronic steps taken that did not result in automated functions):

- Insurance verification capabilities not provided or compromised
- Interface issues

OIG COMPLIANCE ISSUES

The following key items specifically addressed compliance issues and high-risk exposure. The most significant impact was that the

EXHIBIT 8.O	DATA PROFILE: IMPACT ON OPERATIONS EFFICIENCY

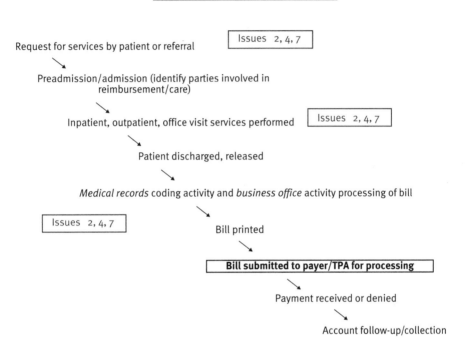

Hospital Inefficiency Impact

Request for services by patient or referral — Issues 2, 4, 7

Preadmission/admission (identify parties involved in reimbursement/care)

Inpatient, outpatient, office visit services performed — Issues 2, 4, 7

Patient discharged, released

Medical records coding activity and *business office* activity processing of bill

Issues 2, 4, 7

Bill printed

Bill submitted to payer/TPA for processing

Payment received or denied

Account follow-up/collection

EXHIBIT 8.P	KEY TO EFFICIENCY ISSUES

Issue Found	Issue Description
Issue 1	Never implemented due to contract issues
Issue 2	EHR system never provided
Issue 3	Not part of vendor system
Issue 4	Never reviewed, tested, trained
Issue 5	Interface issues
Issue 6	No audit trail
Issue 7	Never worked
Issue 8	Data integrity

CEO of the hospital reported after initiating implementation of the software that he was unable to verify financial accuracy.

- The contracted services called for a total of 1,012 functions; 452 were implemented or involved attempted implementation. The remaining functions were never initiated due to numerous issues.
- As a whole, 37.72 percent had no audit trail. The significance of no audit trail would directly impact OIG's compliance guidance of internal controls. The system implemented by the e-Health vendor will only document the last individual who made a change in the system. This is a significant system issue because an audit trail of any financial or clinical activity cannot be tracked appropriately for any type of investigation or quality control activity.
- As a whole, 35.74 percent had data integrity issues. Again, this presents significant internal control issues with respect to accurately representing an episode of care from a reimbursement perspective.

GENERAL AUDIT FINDINGS

During the audit process it is important to obtain information on the components of the operational software along with work flows association it with implementation schedules. In addition, specific deficiencies were noted along with an analysis of the damages to the hospital. The following is an example of issues that were addressed within the audit report.

1. During the analysis of any type of operational software, a process flowchart of design/implementation areas should be completed prior to designing and implementing a new system. The auditor never received any preliminary analysis from the EHR vendor. Exhibit 8.Q illustrates the accounts receivable pipeline for a provider.
2. EHR systems must be prepared to handle complex potential reimbursement methodologies to process accounts receivable. EHR vendors should analyze reimbursement methodology diversity by performing a *payer mix analysis*. In other words, providers must understand the diversity of payer activity that occurs at their facility. The auditor never received any payer mix analysis from the EHR vendor.

EXHIBIT 8.Q   **ACCOUNTS RECEIVABLE PIPELINE**

Accounts Receivable Pipeline

Request for services by patient or referral

Preadmission/admission (identify parties involved in reimbursement/care)

Inpatient, outpatient, office visit services performed

Patient discharged, released

Medical records coding activity and *business office* activity processing of bill

Bill printed

Bill submitted to payer/TPA for processing

Payment received or denied

Account follow-up/collection

3. Exhibit 8.R illustrates a sample data identification map, typically produced during the assessment phase prior to the implementation of a new software system. At minimum, a data map of the hospital should have been prepared for the EHR functions that correlated to the request for proposal. The auditor never received any analysis of the hospital's data layout from the EHR vendor.

4. Implementation of new software without consideration for operational pipelines often leads to clinical and financial data integrity issues that may impact both quality of care and revenue. A lack of data integrity might also impact management of the business infrastructure and the staff associated with the delivery of that business function, including direct and indirect patient care. Implementation of new software without consideration for reimbursement methodologies can result in compliance and lost revenue issues. Implementation

EXHIBIT 8.R   SAMPLE DATA MAP

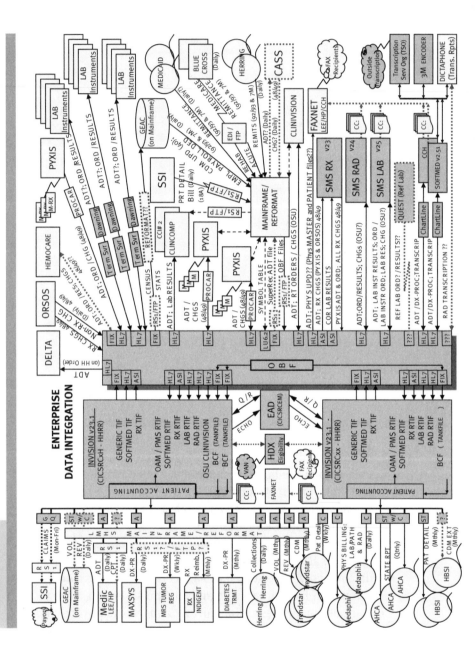

of new software without consideration of activities within a data map can cause significant interface issues.

5. In totality, the EHR contract called for 837 "must-have" functions. Of these, the billing patient financial services had a total of 86 functions; 42 never worked and 44 were implemented but still required many manual functions. Collections accounts receivable had a total of 32 functions; 16 never worked and the 14 implemented still required many manual functions. On average, each function experienced 1.55 issues.

6. At the committed completion date of implementation, 55 percent of the functions were not initiated.

7. Inpatient revenue dropped by more than 5 percent.

8. Based on the OIG compliance guidelines, the hospital appropriately disengaged from a program that was not generating accurate billing statements.

9. The lack of system audit trails adversely impacted the hospital's ability to initiate appropriate financial and clinical internal controls. A lack of internal control can impact patient safety and carry financial repercussions from third-party payers. The most recent HIPAA provisions include private-payer programs as well as public programs.

10. A lack of data integrity adversely impacted the hospital's ability to maintain quality of care and accurate charge capture. A lack of data quality can impact patient safety as well as generate over- and undercharges to third-party payers.

DAMAGES

During the course of the audit, benchmark information was collected. A methodology was outlined to determine and measure actual damages, and the following assessment was incorporated into the audit:

1. Significant "must-have" software deliverables were not implemented and not available on the EHR system.

2. The hospital suffered a multimillion-dollar loss in net inpatient revenues as a result of the agreed-on not-functional "must-have" processes.

3. The hospital suffered more than a quarter of a million dollars in labor costs associated with inpatient activity to mitigate nonfunctional aspects of the EHR system.

4. The hospital suffered a loss of over a million dollars in net outpatient revenues as a result of the agreed-on not-functional "must-have" processes.

5. The hospital suffered almost half a million dollars in labor costs associated with outpatient activity to mitigate nonfunctional aspects of version 4 software.

6. Total operational damages were noted at almost $5 million dollars.

AUDIT IMPLICATION OVERVIEW

Buyers beware! EHR offerings in the marketplace are numerous and sophistication varies significantly among vendors. Auditors must recognize how market players interact with each other. Within one entity, the transfer and modification of an e-health environment can be costly and compromise an organization significantly if careful planning and testing does not occur. The internal auditor's role is to ensure reliability of the offering, benchmark against market standards, and the implementation and continue with ongoing testing of internal controls to preserve defined functionality. The e-health systems in this chapter are discussed from the perspective of the stakeholder using the software during the course of its business process. The next chapter focuses on the EHR systems from a patient perspective.

ENDNOTES

1. http://www.nubc.org/.
2. http://www.whitehouse.gov/omb/egov/documents/domain1.doc.
3. http://www.ccrstandard.com

CHAPTER 9

Healthcare Portfolio

Everything changes, nothing remains without change.

—BUDDHA (563 B.C.–483 B.C.), FOUNDER OF BUDDHISM

A *portfolio* is a portable case containing loose files and papers. A *healthcare portfolio* contains a file of patient health information or a personal health record. Market offerings for individual personal healthcare record systems are rapidly emerging. They vary in scope, format, structure, and delivery. The Centers for Medicare and Medicaid (CMS) has initiated its own pilot of a personal health record for Medicare beneficiaries:

> In June 2007, CMS initiated a new pilot project to encourage Medicare beneficiaries to take advantage of Internet-based tools to track their health care services and provide them with other resources to better communicate with their providers. The project is expected to run for eighteen months and will enable certain beneficiaries to access and use a Personal Health Record (PHR) provided through participating health plans, and accessible through www.Mymedicare.gov. CMS will collect data to assess the use, usability, and feature preferences of the tools.[1]

In addition, CMS has released the following comments regarding PHRs:

> The Personal Health Record (PHR) is an adjunct tool related to the provider based electronic medical record. In its ideal form, it would be a lifelong resource of health information used by individuals to make health care decisions, and to enable them to share information with their providers. While a uniform, standard definition does not yet exist of a PHR,

consistent applications for PHRs are beginning to emerge. The ideal is for a PHR to provide a complete summary of an individual's health and medical history with information gathered from many sources, including self entries. Personal Health Records will have stringent controls to protect the privacy and security of the information, and individuals will have control over who has access to the information. Today, Personal Health Records are offered by health plans, providers, and independent vendors. Standards are being developed and the tools will continue to evolve along with all of the health information technologies under way.[2]

PHRs are a first stepping-stone toward empowering individual patient-consumers. Current market offerings mainly act as data repositories versus an interactive tool for self-advocacy. MBA's electronic PHR, PortFolia[sm], provides health information when patients need it. Inadequate access to accurate health information at the moment required causes problems for patients. Why is access such a problem? First let's quickly review the healthcare continuum from a slightly different perspective. Numerous challenges in managing patient health information exist because of the fragmented nature of our healthcare system. Exhibit 9.1 illustrates the lack of interoperability within healthcare.

EXHIBIT 9.1   HEALTHCARE CONTINUUM—PHR PERSPECTIVE

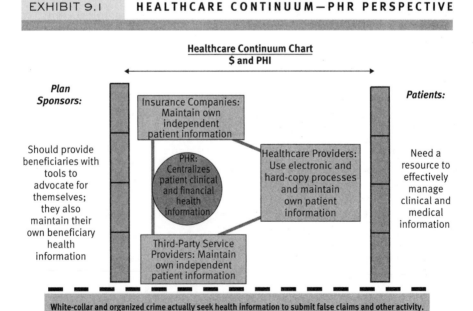

Fragmentation occurs because patients see multiple providers. Providers are not equipped with a centralized database to help them organize comprehensive patient health information and therefore face the cumbersome challenge of exchanging healthcare information among themselves. As a result, ineffective management of personal and financially related health information can cause substandard care and poor healthcare decisions by providers and their patients. Difficulty in exchanging patient health information also subjects patients to a higher risk of medical errors, financial errors, and delayed treatment.

In addition, because the healthcare industry does not separate financial from clinical case management (as discussed in Chapter 3), financial constraints may cause patients to receive delayed, limited, reduced, or no clinical care. As a matter of good faith, providers should be required to separate financial from clinical case management.

As e-health and patient-centric care evolve, patients need a resource to effectively manage their financial and medical information. Healthcare providers continue to use hybrid solutions for their medical records, blending paper and electronic information formats. Insurance companies tend to collect their own files on patients for information relevant to their business needs. Employer plan sponsors similarly maintain only relevant health information on their employees. Numerous third-party players within the healthcare continuum also keep patient files of one sort or another.

Healthcare is a very complex environment. As illustrated in the audit guidelines and market discussion throughout this book, healthcare has significant issues to address outside of access to information and the delivery of healthcare services. First, we must recognize that medical errors do occur. According to the Agency for Healthcare Research and Quality, the price tag for medical errors is about $37.6 billion, or about $4.3 million per hour.[3] Financial errors also occur. Much of public research on financial errors is limited to those generated by providers. Little research, however, has been done regarding financial errors caused by other market players, for example, payer processing claims, pharmacy benefit manager rebate mishandling, and other issues recognizable under employer benefit plan expense reviews. With respect to providers, CMS has released reports for financial errors in the range of $108 billion dollars, or about $12.3 billion per hour. Healthcare fraud schemes' annual price range according to the National Center for Policy and Analysis and BCBS is $83 billion, or about $9.4 million per hour.

PortFolia^sm provides a retrospective, concurrent, and prospective tool for analytics and patient self-advocacy. MBA's PHR originated out of MBA's patient volunteer work. MBA volunteers its time to individual consumers who get stuck in the healthcare system. Long before any market discussion of a PHR or active e-health initiatives, MBA used its audit tools to help individual patients organize and utilize health information for a purpose defined by the patient. Information was organized to mitigate a current issue and prevent future errors. MBA's PortFolia^sm has developed into a comprehensive action-driven private, portable, personal diary and blueprint of health and related financial information. Key system functions:

- Collect all of a patient's medical records and health-, insurance-, and financially related information—all the materials involved in a patient's healthcare experience—in one central, easily accessible, secure resource.
- Enable patients to allow restricted access to share health information with providers to enhance the quality and consistency of care.
- Prepare customizable reports explaining the *who, what, when, where, why*, and *how* of a healthcare episode at any given time.
- Include manual and electronic management and analysis of clinical and health financial information.
- Alert patients to any anomalies with respect to healthcare and financial episodes.

In 20 years of advocating for individual consumers, I have found that, even with the advent of well-crafted patient tools, patients need some type of ongoing resource support. Because of healthcare's continuous dynamic changes, it can be difficult for patients to stay current with market issues. Furthermore, once a patient becomes afflicted with extensive health issues, the volume and magnitude can be overwhelming. The way the healthcare marketplace is structured, it is prohibitively difficult for some patients to obtain, understand, and use the meaningful information needed to make sound healthcare choices. Some type of role in the healthcare marketplace therefore is needed fill this void. Some refer to such a position as an *infomediary specialist*.[4]

Health Infomediary Support

The health infomediary specialist will play an important role as e-health evolves as a dedicated unbiased advocate for the patient. These individuals should be trained and certified to provide support to patients who have difficulty obtaining, understanding, and using meaningful information to facilitate sound healthcare choices. Health infomediary specialists might help patients identify the necessary information to:

- Interpret medical and related financial documents.
- Prepare insurance appeals and fight denials.
- Choose between care alternatives.
- Interact with providers, insurance companies, and benefit plan managers.
- Protect patient interests under the Patient Bill of Rights.

A common openly discussed concern among patients is insurance company denial handling. I find that providers do not effectively track patient employer types, and many patients and providers waste time appealing claims incorrectly. For example, a patient covered by a self-insured employer is subject to ERISA. A patient who is employed by an employer buying health insurance is subject to the state department of insurance. An effective infomediary specialist would need a thorough understanding of the dynamics of each market player from an operational, functional, reimbursement, and clinical perspective.

PHR Attributes

The market will continue to evolve content, privacy, functionality, and security standards for PHRs. PHR usability, however, is also important. PHRs that act solely as data repositories miss fundamental usability opportunities. The standards discussed in this chapter complement basic marketplace initiatives and are driven from an audit perspective and understanding of the healthcare continuum. MBA's PortFolia^{sm} enables patients and their loved ones to monitor and maintain their health and avoid adverse experiences. Prevention and mitigation should be functional components of every PHR. PHRs should also account for a comprehensive picture of patient medical history to allow providers to offer treatment suggestions with access to the whole story. A comprehensive patient medical history includes personal health information, personal healthcare financial management information, and personal documents and research information. Most current data repository systems are not structured to achieve this goal.

PHRs should also demonstrate tangible proof of patient health status and prior health services, and allow providers the opportunity to obtain information that patients may not think relevant. A common misconception is that patients have the skill set to obtain and document all relevant information. I experienced patient frustration, misdirection, and confusion with many of my advocacy patients. For instance, "Dina," the 56-year-old cancer survivor referred to throughout this book, revealed to me that at least three other family members had also experienced interoperative awakening in the past. In all of her family discussions, it never occurred to her that this would be relevant to her situation.

Exhibit 9.2 illustrates the original intent of MBA's PHR program. It also illustrates a simple auditor checklist for patient advocacy:

- Aggregate the relevant health data.
- Identify the problem.

EXHIBIT 9.2   **ORIGINAL PHR MISSION**

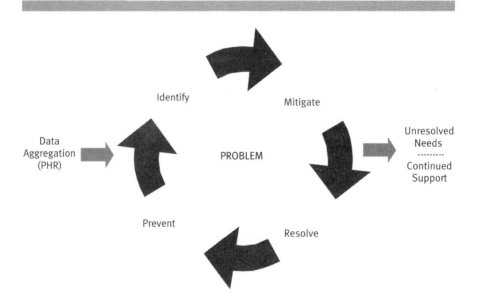

- Determine mitigation options.
- Resolve the problem.
- Prevent the problem from occurring again.
- Document other unresolved needs.
- Determine appropriate needs for continued support.

The process of data aggregation collects all patient health information into one secure place, creating a data repository. Exhibit 9.2 illustrates an audit process to address specific patient issues. One might consider this deviation evolutionary in comparison with current PHR offerings. However, MBA's process has since further evolved. To prepare patients to address and handle ongoing issues, the centralized focus on a *problem* as a trigger point had to move outside the process cycle. MBA's next-generation PHR, PortFolia[sm], adopts the following process cycle, illustrated in Exhibit 9.3, to help patients manage their healthcare consumption.

Patient access to health information when it is needed requires managing consumption in real time regardless of any presenting issue. Most important, patients can stay informed and involved in their care. Together, patients and effective PHRs will enable and empower patient self-advocacy. Patient ability to self-advocate will minimize risk and exposure to medical errors, financial errors, and fraud schemes.

EXHIBIT 9.3   PHR MISSION THAT MANAGES HEALTHCARE CONSUMPTION

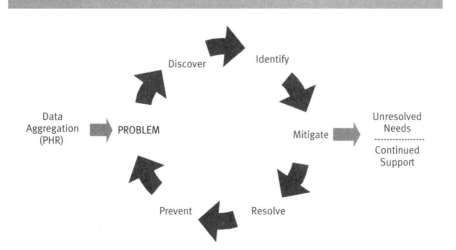

Having an option for provider access and transfer of patient health information is another important attribute for an effective PHR. This function breaches new technological territories but will ultimately facilitate interoperability. Nevertheless, patients with information in hand who actually point things out to their providers such as "Wait—you already did that test on me!" are a valuable commodity.

FUTURE CONSIDERATIONS

Individuals need to become better healthcare consumers to improve the quality and efficiency of our healthcare system. This means that patients and all of us who work in healthcare need to take proactive measures to protect against waste, fraud, and abuse. Using PHRs and infomediary support specialists as resources, patients will be able to effectively manage and control their healthcare experience. Tools such as PortFolia[sm] will empower patients and their loved ones to take charge of their healthcare experience and information for longer, more productive lives. They will improve healthcare decisions and enhance care, condition, disease, and related financial management.

The marketplace also needs to improve patient health by making it easier for patients and families to stay healthy through informed health monitoring. Without informed monitoring and the development of strategic organization of health information, it is difficult to avoid medical errors. The marketplace also needs to provide tools to help patients avoid financial errors. This includes teaching patients how CPT (procedures) and ICD (diagnosis) codes work. Informed patients will help avoid erroneous and lost health and related financial information through systematic record-keeping procedures. In fact, patient education should also complement any PHR initiatives. PHRs should also promote informed healthcare decisions by explaining patient rights and providing diagnosis information and relevant healthcare news.

In time, PHRs should include the following attributes:

- Collect all of a patient's medical records and health-, insurance-, and financially related information—all the materials involved in a patient's healthcare experience—in one central, easily accessible, secure resource.
- Enable patients to allow restricted access to share health information with providers to enhance the quality and consistency of care.

- Explain the *who, what, when, where, why,* and *how* of a healthcare episode at any given time.
- Include manual and electronic management and analysis of clinical and health financial information.
- Alert parties of any anomaly with respect to healthcare and financial episodes.
- Demonstrate tangible proof of patient health status and prior health services and allow providers the opportunity to obtain information that patients may not think relevant.
- Store all patient health information in one secure place—easily accessible for routine doctor visits or a sudden onset of a new health problem.
- Help patients stay informed and involved in their care, enabling and empowering educated healthcare consumers, thereby minimizing risk and exposure to medical errors, financial errors, and fraud schemes.
- Deliver the electronic medical documentation/record that providers and doctor groups have long supported.
- Allow providers access to secure patient healthcare information to support patient visits.
- Enable providers to avoid duplicate or unnecessary tests and procedures, saving money and lives.

MAJOR MARKET ACTIVITY

Several major players have taken the initiative to develop PHRs. Employer groups are driven by the ever-increasing cost of providing benefits and are actively seeking online solutions through various avenues. Insurance companies are also exploring their own answers but tend to offer limited solutions. Providers are developing programs that tend to be limited by their internal infrastructure and their own scope of service offerings. They seem to address only financial and technical constraints in their EHR systems. A number of cottage-industry market players are also launching various forms of data repository tools. These PHR offerings do not include interactive tools that make the PHR a usable and productive self-empowerment tool. Exhibit 9.4 highlights the current status of the marketplace.

EXHIBIT 9.4   **PHR MARKET ACTIVITY**

PHR Capability Analysis	Data Repository	Health Research	Clinical Case Management	Financial Case Management	Error and Fraud Detection Training	Market Expertise	Patient Centric	Certified Advocate Specialist Support
Ideal PHR	x	x	x	x	x	x	x	x
Government	TBD	TBD	TBD			Developing		
Employers	TBD	TBD	TBD					
Insurance companies	x	Limited	Limited	Limited		Developing		
Providers	x	x	x			Developing		
E-Health information resources	x	x	x			Developing	x	
Cottage industry	x		x			Developing	x	

AUDIT IMPLICATION OVERVIEW

Auditors should appreciate the development of EHR business solutions throughout the healthcare continuum and how many market players are attempting to offer various forms of patient PHR tools. For the time being, many EHR offerings should be classified as "hybrid solutions," in the sense that some part will be electronic and some will be paper. As a result, patients will continue to struggle to aggregate data. That aside, in an environment without content standards, the key operative audit issue remains the *interoperability* of any of these independent system offerings.

ENDNOTES

1. http://www.cms.hhs.gov/PerHealthRecords/.
2. Ibid.
3. http://www.ahrq.gov/qual/errback.htm.
4. Jim Adams, *Healthcare 2015 and U.S. Health Plans* (New York: IBM Corporation, 2007), p. 24.

CHAPTER 10

Conclusions

Be not the first by which a new thing is tried, or the last to lay the old aside.

—ALEXANDER POPE (1688–1744), ENGLISH POET AND SATIRIST

MARKET OVERVIEW

Let's take this opportunity to recap some of the key concepts addressed in the previous nine chapters. The first concept discussed in Chapter 1, and illustrated again for convenience in Exhibit 10.1, was the P-HCC.

The S-HCC, introduced in Chapter 1 and reillustrated in Exhibit 10.2, was the second major concept introduced.

Both P-HCC and S-HCC market players generate, process, and use health information independently and simultaneously. For example, a provider may notice an outbreak of a certain disease and report disease information to a public health agency. The provider likely generates both patient-specific health data and health data aggregated from patients with similar outbreaks. Once data is sent to a public health agency, the agency likely generates, processes, and exchanges three different health files: one to identify the provider, another to identify the affected patient, and a third to identify other providers who are reporting similar patient conditions. The Information Continuum (IC), reillustrated in Exhibit 10.3, addresses the technology infrastructure that hosts these types of health information transactions.

EXHIBIT 10.1   **PRIMARY HEALTHCARE CONTINUUM PLAYERS**

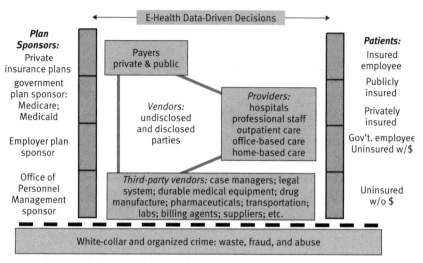

Source: MBA Inc. (www.mbanews.com; copyright 2007).

EXHIBIT 10.2   **SECONDARY HCC MARKET PLAYERS**

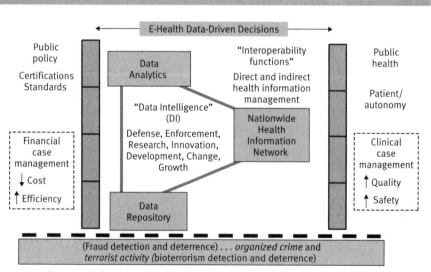

Source: MBA Inc. (www.mbanews.com; copyright 2007).

EXHIBIT IO.3   INFORMATION CONTINUUM (IC)

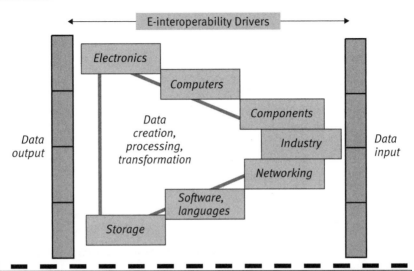

Segmented, Fragmented, Insulated, Non-par Application and Pace

Source: MBA Inc. (www.mbanews.com; copyright 2007).

Understanding these three continuums provides auditors the following conceptual framework:

- The primary HCC, consisting of the major market players including the patient, provider, payer, plan sponsor, and third-party vendors, as well as white-collar and organized criminals
- The secondary HCC, consisting of various support roles and users of heath information that do not provide direct or indirect patient care
- The IC, which provides a systems perspective of the P-HCC and S-HCC

Auditors can use this framework to answer any e-health issues related to the following questions:

- What types of changes are market players introducing? *(To monitor the IC continuum)*

- How will market players achieve these changes and manage the existing environment while in transition? *(To monitor industry application and standards)*
- How will these changes affect our current healthcare system? *(To monitor the P-HCC and the S-HCC)*
- Why are these changes taking place? *(e.g., high exposure to errors, waste, fraud, and abuse)*
- How is information used internally, within a particular market player, and once it leaves, within the entire healthcare continuum?

Market Standards

Chapter 2 introduced the evolving e-health market standards developed by CMS and other independent organizations. The key standards presented address networking, interoperability, system infrastructure, content, and security capabilities. Recognizing e-health market standards enables auditors to examine the effects of a particular market player's infrastructure from both an internal and external perspective. For instance, providers must take into account related payer industry standards when developing any internal system changes. The following list rehighlights the resources that auditors should use as a base when developing a market standard reference list:

- Agency for Healthcare Research and Quality (AHRQ), www.ahrq.gov
- National Resource Center for Health Information Technology, healthit.ahrq.gov
- The Office of the National Coordinator for Health Information Technology (ONC), www.hhs.gov/healthit/
- "Recommended Requirement for Enhancing Data Quality in Electronic Health Records," www.hhs.gov/healthit/
- Health Level Seven (HL7), www.hl7.org
- American National Standards Institute (ANSI), www.ansi.org
- Certification Commission for Healthcare Information Technology (CCHIT), www.cchit.org
- Department of Defense Records Management Program (DOD Directive 5015.2), www.defenselink.mil/webmasters/
- Association of Records Managers and Administrators (AMRA), www.amra.org

E-health is not limited to the United States; it is a worldwide activity. Remember that in today's international community, we have international employers, employees, and travelers. Auditors should also appreciate evolving standards worldwide. How will we effectively manage a patient working one week in the United States and the next week in India? The PHR will become a significant tool in helping this type of patient.

E-health continues to develop and transform at a swift pace. Auditors should expect today's environment to become obsolete within the next 10 years. The audit process in e-health requires contemporaneous management of current infrastructure while preparing for ongoing updates and changes to the environment. Auditors therefore should also expect to invest heavily in research in preparation for auditing e-health system infrastructures and resources.

Market Conflicts

One of the fundamental flaws in healthcare is the lack of separation between clinical and financial issues. Chapter 3 presented critical areas of conflict that exist when decisions appear to be clinical but are driven by financial conflicts of interests. As previously discussed, clinical decisions should be made independently of financial decisions. Auditors should provide reasonable assurance that the current procedures do not allow financially driven conflicts of interest to affect clinical decisions. The development of virtual case management models (VCM) should be conscious of separating financial case management of a patient (FCM) from clinical case management (CCM) of a patient while interacting in the VCM environment. This reorganization will set the stage for developing conflict-of-interest controls throughout the healthcare continuum.

Market Intelligence

In Chapter 4, data in an e-health environment is all about opportunity for efficient and effective decision making. The audit perspective involves testing the integrity of the electronic data and its use in defined algorithms. Does the algorithm ascend to data-driven, intelligence-based outcomes? What are the internal controls to ensure the integrity of the processing and use of the data elements and their transmissions? Integrating internal control into the data-testing process allows for reasonable assurance of data integrity in the financial, operational, and service sectors of e-healthcare environments.

As e-health moves forward, the creation and analysis of algorithms used by market players will require an understanding of how information is generated. Furthermore, to create effective process algorithms, clinical and financial attributes of health data will need to emerge. In addition, in order to achieve interoperability, transactions that were not transparent in the past will be challenged as they become apparent. Money has always been and will continue to be a sensitive issue. Expect barriers to progress to appear when financial matters affecting bottom lines arise. In the meantime, the marketplace can and should establish two distinct disciplines: financial and clinical case management.

One fundamental attribute of e-health is its ability to create constructive, usable, intelligent data. The management of data has become a skill set in the world of e-health. Auditors can provide value by developing data-driven intelligence-based internal controls. The integrating of internal controls into the data-testing process allows for reasonable assurance of data integrity in the financial, operational, and service sectors within the P-HCC and S-HCC. Chapter 5's discussion of algorithms and their capabilities explored how auditors can use a variety of algorithms and data routes to help create an optimal e-health environment. Chapter 6 then explored how the creation of constructive, intelligent, usable data enables effective data-driven decisions, and provided sample applications from the patient, provider, payer, and plan sponsor perspective. Chapter 6 also provided additional examples of data-driven decision applications within the S-HCC, the pharmaceutical industry, and white-collar and organized crime.

Market Audits

Organizations deciding to invest in new electronic health record (EHR) systems or initiate modifications to a current system in the rapidly changing environment of e-health need to take caution. Chapter 7 provided an overview of analytic tools and auditor checklist considerations in auditing e-health. The discussion on market player business processes for consideration is critical when transforming to an e-health environment. Most likely this will occur incrementally. During this transformation, it is important to identify the critical entities in the delivery and payment processing of healthcare services in the primary healthcare continuum. This is followed by looking at market factors that impact these entities in the secondary healthcare continuum. The information continuum identified the e-health infrastructure for these entities and market factors. We then explored data, how to manage data through algorithms, and its impact on the decision-making process. This chapter highlighted the business processes in which data-driven decisions occur.

Chapter 8's case study examined what can go wrong when buying decisions are made without proper testing and verification. The recovery from a bad conversion can be devastating to any organization. Not only are clinical and financial outcomes affected, but so are the processes that employees must carry out. In addition, this chapter provided insight into how current e-health vendor tools vary significantly from just two of the market players. The tools for payers vary significantly from the tools offered to providers. Yet these two market players are expected to achieve interoperability. Market entities that are developing e-health standards should take into consideration the current "business environment" and how those entities vary from a data perspective.

Market Directions

Electronic health records directly benefit those market players that generate or use health information to provide or play a support function in providing patients with healthcare services and products. Personal health records (PHRs), however, directly benefit the patient's own system for managing health information. Eventually, each market player will use its own EHR system to meet its own business demands. In theory, in an interoperable e-health environment, health data should seamlessly transfer to a patient's PHR. Chapter 9 offered additional standards for systems to channel PHR. In essence, these standards suggest a second-generation PHR concept. Today, the market is still developing first-generation tools, but in the near future, it will be important to establish how specific EHR systems can interact or connect with individual PHRs. Exhibit 10.4 suggests an integration point for EHR and PHR systems.

If the PHR is to be the final resting place for an individual's health information, a truly interoperable healthcare environment will need to be created: transparency among and between market primary and secondary

EXHIBIT 10.4   **EHR AND PHR INTEGRATION**

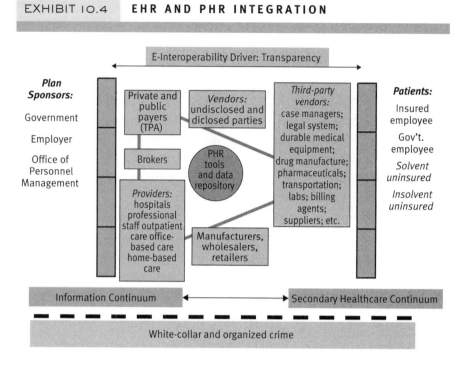

market players; portability standards; data element and content standards; information aggregation, maintenance, processing, and exchange standards must be developed; and the required technological infrastructures must be created.

CONSUMER RESPONSE TO PHRS

The *Wall Street Journal* released a survey finding of consumer responses to the benefits of electronic health records. They included 2,153 U.S. adults in their study, which noted some of the following statistics:[1]

- 75 percent of respondents believe that patients would receive better care if doctors and researchers were able to share information more easily via electronic transactions.
- 63 percent believed medical errors would be reduced.
- 55 percent believed it would reduce healthcare costs.
- 25 percent use some type of electronic medical record.

In preparing some final notes for this book, I decided to conduct my own survey. I included a range of professionals and stay-at-home parents. I was interested is some free-form narrative responses. The process generated some very interesting comments. One response from a non health-care professional read as follows "URGENT—Now that I answered your survey, tell me if the average Joe, not working in healthcare, knows what you are talking about!" The response is a gentle reminder to industry professionals to not forget the most important stakeholder—the patient.

I also talked with attorneys who represent clients in workers' compensation and personal injury cases. One attorney's first response to the idea of e-health reflected his experience with his clients: "I cannot tell you the number of times in which I have clients shocked at what is contained within their medical records. The reality of what is written and documented within their records comes to them as a shock. In particular, when sensitive, very personal, emotionally intimate items are discussed. The first question they ask is if they can block that information." In fact, my survey revealed that not one person owned a complete copy of their medical records to review. Another interesting commentary about the legal system is the notion that once patients become involved in litigation, their rights to privacy are "waived" or lost. The concept that an individual who needs to utilize the civil or criminal process to self-advocate must relinquish his or her privilege to privacy should put a privacy activist on alert.

The next survey questions are followed by particular responses that will represent the range of responses or raise one or more significant insights not addressed in other responses:

1. Do you know what a personal electronic health record is?
    - A record of a person's history of health kept on a computer. It can track if something changes dramatically so that you can become more aware of a problem quicker.
    - I don't know for sure. I'm assuming it's a disk/electronic device or something that would hold all your health information.
    - An online format of your health records that has everything available for a doctor to view in case of emergency.
    - I have no idea.
    - Electronic health records are stored on the computer and can be shared with other health professionals and insurance companies if

need be. They are a more efficient way to store records, but the concern as always is patient privacy.

- It is a repository in electronic form of all relevant health information related to an individual, including diagnoses, allergies, medications, surgeries, physician notes, radiology and lab results, and other relevant medical information.
- A place to store all your medical info. Provides easy access to your records.
- My health record but in an electronic format so that each doctor that I visit would see the same medical history. It would most likely make things easier for the doctors because the patient would not be leaving any details out.
- A record of a person's medical history kept on a computer file. It would be kept up to date and available to a healthcare provider if the patient consents.
- The "flip" answer would be that it computerizes healthcare records, speeding the ability to document badly and spread the errors more broadly, rapidly, and efficiently for the benefit of all parties except the patient.
- It stores your health data.
- It enables ambulatory care physicians and clinical staff to document patient encounters, streamline clinical workflow, and securely exchange clinical data with other providers, patients, and information systems.
- An electronic health record allows people to keep track of their own records.
- The VA hospitals are on top of that. A computerized record that enables each specialist to cross-check treatment and medications in a patient.
- One-stop shopping for my medical history.
- A record kept online for access from any computer. I can keep track of all of my healthcare information, and those who need it can access it when they need to.
- It is an electronic record of my healthcare activity provided by the doctor, laboratory, etc., to be used instead of just a paper chart.
- It provides an electronic history of my healthcare activity with my doctor, labs, imaging, etc.

2. Whom would you want to host your personal health record and why? (Sample options of insurance company, hospital, professional, and third party were provided.)

- I would prefer to have my personal physician host it and allow it to change with personal care physicians because the track record is personal. If something changes, I would rather know from a doctor, not an insurance company.

- Certainly *not* my insurance company or a hospital. Seeing that many people have different doctors, I would believe a third party/professional or myself. I don't trust insurance companies at all. People see different doctors and go to different hospitals for different things, so it wouldn't make sense for them to manage the information. The best host, I would guess, is me.

- Insurance company.

- Never the insurance company, because they may use the information to weed out unhealthy patients. I would want the records held by my doctor or the hospital as they are using the information to help care for me.

- I would prefer that my electronic personal health record be hosted by my hospital. I know that the hospital has to comply with HIPAA and the OIG is looking at intrusion. In addition, most hospitals have disaster recovery plans and backup plans in emergency situations. I would be more comfortable knowing that my hospital has controls in place than a third party that is more susceptible to intrusion from the outside.

- A third party that could communicate with hospitals, doctors, insurance companies.

- Would prefer the doctor to host it due to privacy issues.

- Third party—so that I can truly administer.

- I am not sure. Not the insurance company. Not the hospital; I would feel that it could be accessed too easily. Perhaps a third party that specialized in this, or my private doctor. In many ways, I would want to keep a hold of it myself.

- I believe physicians should have a database where they could enter information easily with each visit, the same way they write in your chart or record when you visit them. Also, with each inpatient or outpatient hospital visit, the hospital could also forward your medical records to that common database. I can see potential for error in any system that would organize medical records.

- I prefer to host it myself. All others have incentives to use it for their purposes, which may not align with my best interests.
- Doctor only, with restrictions on whom he or she can share information with and only with my oral or written permission to do so.
- Third party and available to those who need it.
- Providers and payers for systematic data management and exchanges.
- Not an insurance company—some stuff perhaps they shouldn't know. They will misuse the data. The only one who needs to track it is myself and my primary—so it should be one of these two people who holds it (or an independent third party that I hire to keep it—I send them the records and I pay them).
- If my insurance company hosted the info, then it would be the most accessible. If you happened to be a party to an incident anywhere in the world, you would most likely have your insurance card on hand and the health provider can look up the info on a database.
- I am not sure, but I imagine it's just a matter of time before they all have access to it, especially if someone can make a buck doing it.

3. Do you keep track of your information now?
   - I go to the doctor once a year for a checkup and that's all the tracking I do. If I need to watch cholesterol, I exercise more. I am fairly healthy!
   - Yes. I have it all filed and recorded.
   - Not really: (
   - I keep all the billing information.
   - I have kept some important x-ray reports or lab work in a file at home.
   - I keep track of my health information that is provided to me manually in a file.
   - No—I rely on my hospital and doctor.
   - Yes—paper file.
   - Not really; I have some lab reports, etc., from the past. I do not have a personal medical record.

- Kind of. I have hardcopy files for each family member. Within each file are folders for each illness they had along with the bills for that illness and one general folder for miscellaneous doctor visits. An example: My son had a broken leg and a shoulder injury two years ago. So in his file for two years ago, he would have a folder for "shoulder injury," one for "leg injury," and one for miscellaneous doctor visits (like sinus infections or minor medical problems). I also keep a folder in each of our files for eye care and dental visits. Though the EOBs mostly make up what is in the folders, I also add medical information that pertains to that particular illness.
- No (thankfully, still simple enough healthcare issues).
- Yes, as a diabetic I monitor my sugar regularly.
- I just keep the RX records on my computer.
- No.
- Don't have any to keep track of.
- I keep track in my head.
4. How confident are you that when you go to see a doctor/healthcare professional, he or she always has an accurate and complete picture of your prior medical history?
   - I am *not* confident. My doctor of over 20 years needed to move to Wisconsin because of malpractice insurance. I trusted her. Now I belong to a family community group in which the doctors change every two or three years after they graduate and move on. I know my previous medical history and thank God that I am healthy and not that concerned!
   - I'm pretty confident that they have a clear picture because I tell them exactly what I have. But I don't believe every doctor/healthcare professional/hospital always listens.
   - Not confident—recently went to the doctor, who couldn't remember all of my dates, immunizations, etc., especially for my children.
   - Not confident.
   - Not at all. That is why I try to present a summary of my case or that of my loved ones in addition to important previous test results and lab data.
   - I only see one doctor, so I am confident the information is complete and accurate.

- Not confident.
- Have gone to the same doc for 14 years, so I feel like he person-ally knows me, but he could still forget some things unless he really digs deep or I remind him.
- Fairly confident if in network—not confident at all if out.
- I am not. I try to stay with the same doctors and/or I try to be as accurate as possible with my medical history. However, mine is not that extensive so it is not so difficult.
- I have had the same MD for 25 years, so she knows our fam-ily pretty well, but perhaps a quick access to a database would be beneficial for the primary MD along with any consulting MDs a patient may need.
- Every year when I have my annual physical, I get a set of forms from my PCP, one of which is a Review of Systems. Every year I include some new finding in the Review of Systems, and I vary it from year to year. To date my PCP has never asked me a single question about the Review of Systems findings, suggesting he's never read it.
- Not much confidence. I always have my own entire history. My experience is, don't assume your doctor knows you that well.
- I am confident that my PCP has a reasonably accurate picture of the important aspects of my personal medical history. However, when assisting in the care of my aged parents (before they died), my brother and I learned we could not be confident that phy-sicians had an accurate picture of important aspects. When they were hospitalized, my brother and I took turns making certain one or the other of us were there in order to make certain that mis-takes (sometimes life-threatening mistakes) were not made in their care. We learned from experience that doctors tended to treat the simple basic picture and had difficulty incorporating important variant information and it was nearly impossible to correct errone-ous information mistakenly documented. (Example: Somewhere along the line, my mother's PCP entered into her record that she had had a heart attack. He never removed that from his record despite my mother, myself, and her cardiologist all providing doc-umentation demonstrating that that information was wrong.)

- I believe they do.
- To the degree I am alert, I can tell them. If I arrived unconscious, then it could be a different story. They need to be updated on major stuff.
- As long as I visit the same provider on a regular basis, I am fairly confident that the info is current.
- I assume they know nothing because that's what I am used to. But lately, they can relay to me exact dates I was last in with the same symptoms, and that's kind of cool, as far as seeing trends.

5. Do you think e-PHRs can reduce the number of redundant or unnecessary procedures and improve healthcare quality?
   - Yes.
   - Absolutely.
   - No.
   - Possibly, because other professionals could see when the individual last had a test done.
   - Don't know—wouldn't think people didn't know what they've had before and could control that.
   - Yes, I could see how they would streamline all different doctors' info and past procedures together.
   - Perhaps, if it was set up in an organized way where the healthcare providers could quickly get the information they were looking for.
   - Possibly, provided that docs use the medical record and really look at all notations made by all docs, RNs, etc.
   - Have not seen the real outcome yet. Theoretically, it should.
   - In theory—assuming accuracy and accessibility it should help. Records are only as good as the record keeper. The concept is a good one. Just like computers can keep track of your taxes, your music, your e-mails, your stock trades—why not all your medical records? I would be interested in software to store this for myself in my house on my computer.
   - Definitely, as long as those results from those procedures are entered into the database in a timely and accurate manner. That would mean that it would be necessary to have a system in place to automatically enter that info into the files for folks who are

involved in an electronic health record program. It would improve the quality and the continuity of care for those involved.

6. Do you think e-PHRs can significantly decrease the frequency of medical errors and reduce healthcare costs?

   • Yes to the first, because reading the electronic record is easier than some handwriting. No to the second, because e-PHR is not cheap.

   • Errors will occur because humans are running the tests. Incorrectly inputted information can mislead the patient. I think it may decrease, but I think it will raise healthcare costs because of the cost to implement the system.

   • Yes.

   • No.

   • Not necessarily, unless the medications or tests are being reviewed by a third party.

   • Probably.

   • Yes, it seems that they would. Also, I think it would really help those patients who face numerous procedures and illness or who can't speak the language, and/or cannot take care of themselves.

   • I am not sure. It may help with medical errors and healthcare costs, but I personally do not believe having PHRs would have a significant effect on costs. I think other factors influence health-care costs more.

   • It's one way, but not the only means, and I don't think it would significantly reduce errors.

   • Theoretically, yes.

   • I don't know how many medical errors come from inaccurate medical records.

   • As long as the e-PHRs are utilized adequately. (You know how the healthcare system is!) With many providers going electronic, I would imagine this would make it easier for providers to comply with getting all the info into the profile in a timely manner.

7. Do you think patients should have direct access to their own medical record maintained by their physician?

   • Yes. I already know that the orthodontist allows you to view your personal information online.

   • I think everyone should have access to their own medical records.

- Yes
- This may not be a good idea.
- Yes and no—I would like to see my medical record. However, I do think that if doctors knew that patients would see what they wrote after each visit it would affect what they would write. It may be less objective.
- I think patients should have read-only access to their medical records.
- The system should not be for providers only. The patients should have equal access.
- Patients should have access to their medical records.

8. Do you think e-PHRs will make it more difficult to ensure patient privacy? Why?

- Anything online is subject to scams and to vulnerability of information being released without knowledge. I still do not trust the online security system. Therefore, I do not use it.
- Depends on how the information is managed. If I care for my own records, I think that the information is kept mostly private, but I could lose them. That's not to say that some other third party couldn't lose them. Things are lost all the time. Problem is that when things are lost, sometimes they are found by others and what they do with that information is of concern. Also, I think people are finding more ways to break through electronic codes, and that could put someone at risk for exposure. I also think it leaves your whole healthcare open to be viewed by whatever person you're seeing—who may not need to know certain information.
- People try to hide stuff and it might be dangerous, like the types of medicines they may be taking and then getting a procedure, and people forget!
- No.
- Not really. I don't know how secure the paper copies are.
- Yes, depending on how it is maintained. If it is maintained by a third-party vendor online, there can be intrusion and backup issues. If maintained by your hospital electronically, I feel it can be more secure.
- No; someone would have to work pretty hard to get to the information.

- No; this stuff is transmitted all over the Internet now.
- Yes; I would just be afraid that someone could hack into a computer and find out another's personal info. With so much identity theft out there, this could potentially become another form.
- Yes; whenever more people are entering information somewhere, privacy becomes an issue.
- There is always the issue of judgment errors by those who maintain and release information.
- No. Anyway, the benefits far exceed.
- It could result in privacy concerns because more people will access them, even IT supporting staff for the system.
- Absolutely. The pharmaceutical companies would find a way to get information and hound stupid people about taking their cure-all medications.
- Privacy and security are concerns. Hackers, misuse—and I always read about data being wrongly released.
- Probably, because over time the databases will be sold, acquired, and/or merged by larger groups, first local, then community, then regional, and then national.

9. What frustrations do you have with managing your health or that of a loved one? What would help alleviate these frustrations?
    - Frustration occurs only if you do not have a physician whom you can trust or rely on. If you have a good physician, you should not worry about your health. I think people want to micromanage everything and that causes too much stress on the individual. If you have a physician or group of physicians that you trust, then I believe that you will be okay. My aunt recently did not trust any Illinois physicians and went to the Mayo Clinic in Minnesota. She found comfort and was taken care of there. Her trust in the Mayo Clinic was encompassing and she went back for the checkup there. Yes, it was expensive, but for peace of mind it was worth it. If the doctors don't know how to read the medical information provided, they still won't be able to help the patient. The doctors have to be knowledgeable and honest.
    - I have no real frustrations with the management. My frustration is that when I see a new physician very seldom do they look at me as a person who understands my own healthcare. They also, all too frequently, will rerun a test that has been performed before.

As if their test will yield something different, which in my case it never has. It would be helpful if the government would make it illegal for insurance/drug companies to give a doctor *anything* in exchange for "recommending" medicine or doing any other "favor."

- Remembering dates and names of medicines.
- Frustration is with the insurance companies, bad service, billing mistakes, etc.
- There are not enough services for the elderly and there is not enough coverage for drug expenses. We need better home care.
- No.
- Communicating with physicians.
- I am frustrated with my mother's healthcare professionals; they aren't thorough or that familiar with her past medical history.
- Insurance companies—what's covered, what's not, etc.
- At this time, I have no major frustrations—I have more issues with insurance companies. It would be nice, though, to be able to have my whole family's health records streamlined. It would have helped when I lived out of the country.
- You know how a light goes on in your car when it is time for a tuneup? A reminder on a PHR would be helpful. Also, I think it would be helpful for patients to have an area where they could print up helpful forms, for example, a standard form for the medications they are on. That way they could keep it up to date, use it as a tool.
- Most frustrating is the high cost of my insurance premiums.
- Other countries, like Israel, are very successful in centralizing the data with access for the patient and health providers.
- Expensive. Can't get appointments.
- Lack of access to the medical records. Lack of continuity of care. Repetition of all the same information (some people have very lengthy healthcare histories). When I worked in Ambulatory Care and I would begin asking all the health history questions, the patients would get very frustrated and ask "Don't you have all this information already?" I of course would have to answer "no" because unless they were with us previously, there is no continuity of care. The patients would have to repeat all of their info over again, including all of their drug info. I would have to

make several phone calls trying to get recent EKG results, labs, etc. If I could go to one database that included all of their health information and their testing results, this would save so much time and frustration, both for the health provider and the patients. We wouldn't have to bother them as much as we do.

- God has graced us with good health, so it is not an issue presently. The only frustration I would consider is the high cost of private health insurance premiums my friends and family are paying.

10. Would you pay an expert to manage or help manage your healthcare experience to ensure optimal healthcare service?

- Not sure if I could manage it myself—maybe a software program would help.
- No, we need to let doctors do their job and stop adding another layer of professional healthcare service.
- Yes.
- Yes, if I had complete confidence in them; they would have to convince me that my info could not be misused, and I would want to have access to it.
- At the present time, I do not think I would pay someone to manage my family's healthcare information. I am capable of doing that for us. With the high costs of healthcare, I don't know if the consumer would want to spend one more dollar on healthcare. I also believe that the consumer believes it is the healthcare providers' obligation to provide some of these services.
- No, but some seniors who are without family or without active involvement by their families could benefit from such a service.
- It should be a part of the insurance program that you are on.
- In this squeezed generation, taking care of old folks is crazy. I could see people paying someone to get that off their backs. Sift through the mess of all the specialists. Plus, if you have a sick person, just the emotional release of feeling they have someone on their side would probably work.
- No. Too many conflicts of interest. Healthcare concierge— would be just like a hotel concierge—you get sent somewhere by who pays the most, who refers back the most, etc.
- I think it would be an option for an individual to pay for this. As an individual (being an RN), I would pay for this only if

I was certain that the providers would use it. If I were not an RN, I might use it (pay for it) solely to get everything in order. I would think it more reasonable to have a provider, mainly an insurance company or a physician's office, pay for the service. Someone would have to get all of the patient's data in the file after obtaining the info/records, which seems to be the hard part these days. Since the physicians (and nobody else) receive reports on the patient's testing, they seem to be the most obvious folks to keep track of the e-file. I think this would be a nice service for either the insurance companies (they would have to receive all the testing results, though) or really the patient's physician's office to provide for their clients.

- Yes, probably, if I had a potentially fatal disease or health issue.

AUDIT IMPLICATION OVERVIEW

Throughout this book, I have suggested how to approach auditing in an e-health environment. Special attention has been given to certain niche clinical and financial matters. Within the audit of e-health, two customers exist. The first is the organization or entity that is implementing and using an EHR system and the second is the patient and his or her respective PHR. Auditors must remember to listen to their clients—the system users. It is important to recognize users because it is their work product that will make or break the delivery of any good or service.

The survey presented in this chapter is intentionally structured as free-form narrative. The traditional *yes/no* response may facilitate statistical analysis, but the *tone* of the original statements provides for a different kind of understanding. As the market evolves and standards are developed, I hope we do not lose sight of the ultimate stakeholders. The ultimate goal behind the development of an interoperable, cost-effective, transparent, and optimal healthcare environment is to provide market players with effective tools so that they can effectively and reliably service the ultimate customer—the patient.

ENDNOTES

1. Http://online.wsj.com/article_email/article_print?SB11956244262500549-1MyQjQxMD, accessed 11/29/07.

Index